A Small Piece of Africa

Moths of Nyamuluki

Rhodometra
sacraria.
"Vestal"

Sept 75

March '86
Panotenia
prasina.

April 86

Oct 75

Basiothia medea.
"Small Verdant Hawk."

Feb 76
Pericallia ellioti
"Elliots Tiger"

Nov '80. Othreis materna. ♀

July 80

May '81
Celerio lineata
"Striped Hawk"

Dec. '85.
Hypnotion
celerio.
"Silver striped Hawk"

May '81.
Cyligramma latona.
"Cream striped owl"

Gynanisa nigra
"Speckled Emperor."

NJG

NYAMULUKI

A Small Piece of Africa

LAVINIA GRANT

SILENT BOOKS

CAMBRIDGE

First published in Great Britain 1995
by Silent Books Ltd, Swavesey, Cambridge CB4 5QG

© Text and illustration copyright Lavinia Grant 1995

ISBN 1 85183 082 0

British Library Cataloguing-in-Publication Data.
A catalogue record for this book is available from the
British Library.

Typeset by Goodfellow & Egan Ltd, Cambridge
Printed in Hong Kong by Midas Printing

Contents

Acanthaceae.

Thunbergia
alata.

NSG

Thunbergia gregorii.

Introduction

This book is about nature in a patch of Africa I shall call Nyamuluki – a patch so small that it would be passed over in two or three minutes by a high gliding vulture or by a delta-winged bateleur eagle in its endless sweeping search for reptiles. It is a patch of ranching land in the dry bush country north of Mount Kenya and lies on the banks of the Uaso Nyiro River that flows northwards until it disappears in the Lorian Swamp, never to reach the sea.

When I first came to Nyamuluki, I thought it was the most lovely place on earth. People would sometimes ask me how I managed to lived in such an isolated place and if I found it very different from Britain, where I was brought up. The answer is that I have never felt isolated on Nyamuluki for there has been the family – my husband Guy, our three children, Laria, Isabella and Murray – and the ranch and household staff. The landscape seems not so very different from that of the Scottish highlands, which I have always loved, and I feel more at home here than anywhere else.

Murray fishing.

Everything illustrated or mentioned in this book has as its context this comparatively tiny area of land. Only a few miles away, for instance on the other side of neighbouring hills, the weather patterns are quite different. There are tremendous differences of altitude to the north and south which produce climates that range from the cold high moorlands of Mount Kenya in the south, through bamboo, forest, bush and grass-land and the hot semi-desert not too far to the north. All have their own plant and animal communities.

The pictures have been painted from life or from sketches and observations made from life. My paintings of wild flowers are all done from living specimens. If I come upon a new flower while out on a walk I may pick a sprig and bring it home; at other times I have grown plants from seeds or cut-tings in the garden and waited for them to flower. Occasionally I paint the plant where it is growing, out in the bush. I have never used photographs when painting because I have always tried to express a personal feeling about the animals, plants and the places they live in.

I painted the pictures herein for my own interest and for my family, and so this book is far from being a scientific work. There are, I am sure, many inaccuracies and oddities, for it is merely an attempt to communicate something of the variety and beauty of this small piece of Africa.

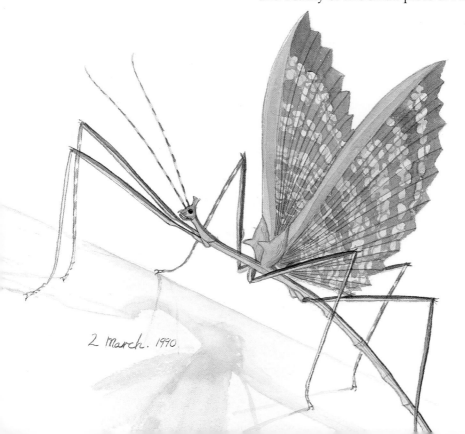

2 March. 1990.

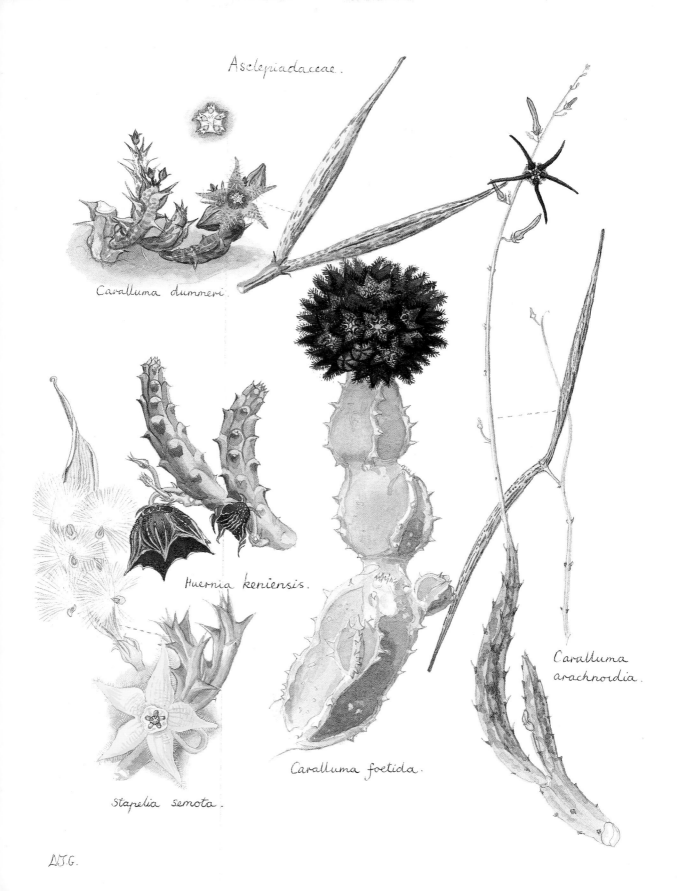

Asclepiadaceae.

Caralluma dummeri.

Caralluma arachnoidia.

Huernia keniensis.

Caralluma foetida.

Stapelia semota.

LJG.

Setaria
pallidifusca.

1.   2.   3.   4.   5.   6.

· 1 ·
The weather and the land

Beyond the craggy and snow-encrusted peak of Mount Kenya is our home Nyamuluki, in a brittle and delicate bushland held in balance by the infinitely subtle hand of nature. At 5,700 feet, Nyamuluki lies in a 'between' land as far as vegetation goes. Many low-altitude plants do not grow here owing to the comparative cold of the nights, and those of higher altitudes which are present, do not obtain the same magnificence as in their truer habitat.

There are two main types of soil within the area of Nyamuluki, each with its distinctive flora. In the south lies a tract of clay called 'black cotton', originating from the lavas of Mount Kenya which was an active volcano within recent geological time. To the north, ancient Archean rock is exposed which has never been covered by sea since dry land was first heaved up out of the primaeval waters. This soil is light, gritty, porous and red, and consists of rotten granite, quartz, iron and glittering mica. When rain falls here the wild flowers often equal or surpass those of an Alpine meadow. Cushions of vivid sky-blue *Pentanisia*, meadows of fawny-pink *Commelina*, stars of yellow and white lilies, drifts of bush violets, the intermittent stitchery of pink vetches and the white and lilac saucers of recumbent bindweeds cover the ground until the earth is embroidered like a heavenly tapestry. The grass here springs fast and sweet, but dries and withers quickly when rain no longer falls.

Pentanisia
ouranogyne.

Commelinaceae

Commelina

Commelina reptans.

Cyanotis foecunda

Commelina africana.

Aneilema hockii

Commelina

By contrast, the southern clay holds its moisture, and the grass there is heavier and thicker, though perhaps less sweet. The trees and bushes are predominantly whistling thorn in the open and mukinyea (*Euclea divinorum*) along the gullies, with scattered *Boscia* trees dotting the whole area. These *Boscia*, or mukuriundu as they are locally known, are characteristic of this country, with their silvery, contorted and knobbly trunks rising to thick green umbrellas spread out on twisted arms above the browse-line of the tallest giraffes. The southern plains present a slightly more monotonous aspect than the country to the north, which is hilly with rocky outcrops and gullies.

Along the river grow larger trees of kinds not found elsewhere, and a luxuriant tangle of characteristic creepers, grasses and herbs clothe the riverbanks. Seeds may be washed down from higher altitudes, and, taking root in the rich silt, flower unfamiliarly for a season or two between clumps of aromatic mint, yellow *Aspilia* daisies and semi-aquatic *Polygonum*. The course of the river is marked from a distance, even in the driest times when the rest of the land is grey and sere, by the green and gold of its willows and fever trees.

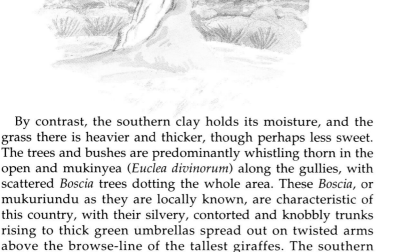

The single most important factor for all living things on Nyamuluki is rain. Everything depends on it, not seemingly indirectly as in temperate lands, but absolutely primarily. Reproduction, growth, and life itself can be sustained from one season to the next only if enough rain falls. There are two seasons – the wet and the dry – which both hold tremendous sway over our lives. We have two dry seasons which are separated by the long rains and short rains. The long rains begin in March, if they are early, and carry on through April and May; the short rains fall in November. Occasionally, light rains, known as the 'lake rains' because they brew over Lake Victoria, fall in August. They are heavy enough to produce a new growth of grass but cannot be counted upon. Occasionally the rains fail altogether, spelling temporary disaster for plants, animals and people alike.

The dry season is the equivalent of winter, when life goes into recess and everything conserves energy. The leaves of the trees are folded along their twigs as protection from the drying sun and wind, and some trees lose their leaves entirely. Plants withdraw into their bulbs and tubers below the baked surface, or entrust their lives to their dry seeds. Grasses live only in their roots. Slowly, the landscape turns tawny, first hazed over with dry grass heads, the green baking away until the grass is almost white. Later it becomes grey and stick-like as the blades wither and drop.

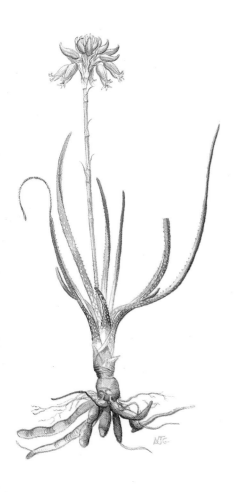

The dry seasons, though at times desolate, have an austere beauty of their own. Perhaps the most beautiful part is toward their end, when it is building up for rain, and the increased humidity has laid the typical dry-weather dust haze. Then the colours of the landscape are both delicate and intense, with clear glass-like tones, as if they have been purified to essences in a white-hot kiln. Clouds begin to form, at first hazy in the simmering blue sky, so that their edges can hardly be discerned, and later in gigantic castles and continents of blazing white.

But the bleakest times occur before the haze settles when the light goes blank and flat, and the plants in the bare, dusty ground, broken and withered to the roots, seem dead. The animals have abandoned the big herds formed in the green season and have spread out over a wider area in their search for food. They seem listless. One wonders what the birds find to eat. Insects seem few and far between, and the ground has been scoured over and over again by flocks of grey-headed social weavers, chestnut sparrows and other seed eaters, and by the pink and grey laughing doves and ring-necked doves who walk slowly and soberly on the hot bare ground.

Before the rains, thorn trees burst into masses of white, cream and yellow blossom, producing the energy and moisture from their stored reserves. Then they come into leaf of a most tender green, which is wonderfully soothing to the eyes. Gradually other signs of change appear. In the gullies, the scarlet flowers of *Crossandra* appear; and the creeping *Justicia* producing its small mauve flowers at the same time making an attractive clash of colour. Under the thorn trees are lemon yellow *Kalanchoë* flowers, often in profusion, borne on tall grey-furred stems. In the blazing sun spiny cushions of *Barleria* are covered with lavender-coloured flowers. Sometimes acres of aloes bloom a month or so before the rain, and the whole area is aflame with their branched heads of coral red and orange. Wild asparagus tendrils, that had hung down limply, now feel upwards, quivering with life. Soon they burst into masses of minute, frothy white flowers, like fountains of milk. In some places every bush is festooned with them. All of this before a drop of rain has fallen, and after months of desiccating wind and sun.

At this time some of the birds, which do not nest all year round like the pigeons and doves, start to sing and display. Young cock sunbirds are getting their first breeding plumage as they chatter excitedly around the new blossom. The white-browed coucal, skulking in the undergrowth, produces its first 'water-bottle' calls in a somewhat hesitant manner. However it is usually right: if the coucal calls, rain is not far off. Ethiopian swallows sing on the wing or from a perch near their intended nest site – rapid canary notes in short varied cadences of great sweetness. But they do not start to build nests, or reline old ones, until the rain actually begins.

In some of the unusually severe dry seasons we have experienced, birds that are not normally seen in this part of the country sometimes appear. Numbers of Hartlaub's turacos move in and take up temporary residence in the heavily bushed gullies, in the garden and along the river. Their crimson wings and moss-green bodies seem to annoy the local turacos, the white-bellied go-away birds, who chase them about the branches with their rubber-duck-like calls, and beat at them with their wings. Swallow-tailed kites come down from the desert north and Somali golden-breasted buntings and flocks of grey-headed silver-bills arrive.

Always before the rains, big, chattering flocks of wattled starlings appear, the males in smart black and pale grey plumage, set off by yellow and black face wattles. These wattles are produced only for the breeding season, which begins with the rain.

Kalanchoe citrina.

Acanthaceae.

Barleria
spinisepela

Crossandra
nilotica.

Barleria
eranthemoides.

Asystasia
gangetica.

Mimosoideae.
Acacia gerrardii.

Inner bark sometimes
used as rope.

July '92.

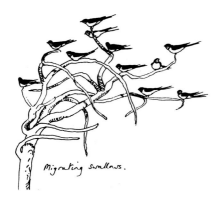

Migrating swallows.

European and Asiatic migrants prepare for their journeys north. The double purring notes of the European bee-eaters fill the air under the mounting cumulus, while great flocks of swallows hesitate, waiting for the rains to produce a harvest of insects to fatten upon before they start their long exodus. Willow warblers, chiffchaffs and sedge warblers haunt the dry bushes unobtrusively, and small flocks of yellow wagtails patter around the feet of cattle and by the river's shallow edges. One broadly moonlit night we heard a migratory nightingale singing, solemn and husky below the excited nocturnal twittering of the local superb starlings, the raucous gull-like calls of crowned plovers and the loud bubbling notes of the spotted stone curlews.

This activity in the birds is stimulated by the rainstorms that have already begun further south. As the humidity builds up, the mornings become very hot. Immaculate citrus swallowtails, orangetips, blues and many other butterflies come out of their chrysalises and bees buzz in the Acacia blossom, frantically building up their stores of honey.

All through the dry weather a strong north wind blows. It gets up during the middle of the morning and by the afternoon it has blown away the promising clouds. While it blows there will be no rain, but when it drops, clouds swirl overhead, waiting to release their moisture. A cool puff of wind coming suddenly from the south is like a messenger with a silver trumpet, for when the wind changes to the south the rains begin. It is the monsoon, the great south-east trade wind turning away the hot desert wind of the north.

Then, one day, the plum-bellied clouds let down their rain in curtains that blot out the horizon and give the earth its first soaking for months. Afterwards the hills are ink-blue and clear as crystal; every particle of dust has been washed from the air, which is full of the delicious smell of wet earth. Birds sing in the release from tension that the rain brings. Stick-like grass stems have softened and give out a smell like new hay. Next day the colour of the landscape has changed imperceptibly and the following day minute spears of green are thrusting up. After the next downpour expanses of brilliant emerald-green onion-grass materialise, and blue and white bush violets (*Craterostigma*) appear in carpets on the shallow soils that overlie rocks.

The rainstorms are exciting, with the rumbling of thunder, and lightning that leaps out of the clouds in sizzling bolts or, at night, fires one end of the horizon or another with almost continuous sheets of flickering light. Then comes the slow, grey

Playing.

Spotted Stone-curlew.
(Burhinus capensis.)

Taking off.

Landing.

About to land.

Habitat on El K.
Small bush on rather
bare ground.

Scratching neck.

Alert with back turned.

Moving off with short runs and stops.

Squatting on "hocks" to be inconspicuous,
with golden eye almost shut.

Almost round egg layed
without nest, on the ground.

SEDGES.

Onion grass.
Cyperus blysmoides.

1.   2.   3.   4.

blotting-out of the landscape as the rain advances and finally arrives, reducing visibility to fifty, then twenty yards. The nearest trees look ghostly, and the ground itself is half hidden in a white mist made from millions of splashes as each rain-drop hits the earth.

Rivulets of water born from spreading puddles, nose their way among stones and tufts of grass, here and there filling impala tracks with small eddies like miniature bowls of tomato soup, each with its frothy swirl of cream. Soon hollows and ditches are flowing with their own brown spates. The gullies collect the water and regular torrents sweep down them to join the river itself, which can swell to six or seven times its usual size when in flood.

The secret dry-weather glades, with their tawny grass, Arthur Rackam-like trees and dusty animal paths winding through woods of leathery-leaved mukinyea, are transformed into green gardens and glens. White and yellow lilies flower suddenly and grass runners spread over the bare places. Natural rock gardens are decorated with small flowers and butterflies. It is all quite magical.

When the rains have started in earnest, activity among the birds is redoubled. Tawny eagles stoop at each other in courtship play, yelping through the sky. Augur buzzards call. D'Arnaud's barbets perch on a bush top and begin their bub-bling monotonous chant, the female holding her tail behind her back and wagging it like a metronome in time to their song. Striped, Ethiopian and mosque swallows collect beakfuls of mud, mix them with rootlets and start to build nests in out-buildings and verandahs. Blue-eared glossy and superb star-lings carry beakfuls of fibres and feathers, like great moustach-es, to secret holes and crannies. There is frantic activity in the Speke's weavers' breeding trees as the little yellow cocks buzz through the air from all directions, trailing long green grass stems with which to weave their nests. They complete these quickly and then the cocks hang upside down beneath them, flapping their wings and wheezing their songs, trying to attact the olive-coloured females to inspect their work. The females poke around inside the nests with their beaks and even push at the walls and ceilings with the tops of their heads, and if not satisfied the cocks build them new nests close by. Cocks and hens together line accepted nests with acacia leaves, grass heads and feathers, the cocks sometimes stealing material from absent neighbours' nests.

Craterostigma plantagineum.

Zebra and eland now congregate, sometimes in very large herds, and followed at foot by many new foals and calves.

Guinea fowl.

Augur buzzard.

Kori bustard.

Spotted eagle owl.

Vulture

Vulture

Augur buzzard

Spiders.

Flat wall-spider.

Egg-cases of the Black Widow spider.

Black Widow ♀

Foreparts of this spider pearly metallic silver.

Underside.

Impala fawns prance gently by their mothers. Six-foot baby giraffes form loose crèches under the watchful eyes of browsing females, who come to feed them at regular, though rather widely spaced, intervals. Jackals play together, wagging their tails like dogs, and produce their litters in burrows and old aardvark holes.

Smaller animals are active too. Sometimes we see a female burrowing spider come to the top of her round hole in the ground, backwards, with masses of brown spiderlings clustered on her abdomen. They sun themselves on their mother's body, or climb nearby grass stems till a gentle breeze blows, when each will exude a loop of gossamer. The breeze lifts this fine strand like a parachute, and each spiderling is carried into the sunny air and flies away, eventually to land and dig itself a minute, round hole and begin its own independent life.

Wasps of many kinds build clay pots in which they immure small spiders or caterpillars which have been paralysed by a sting. On these inert bodies the wasps lay their eggs. Later, when the wasp grubs hatch, they will feed on the fresh meat which surrounds them. Caterpillars of many different kinds change their instars quickly in order to pupate, metamorphose, breed and lay before the dry weather catches up with the next generation. Migrations of butterflies occasionally pass through Nyamuluki like coloured snowstorms, for days on end. Sometimes when conditions are just right, the green and black caterpillars of the army-worm moth appear in vast numbers to eat the grass as hungrily as locusts. Areas that should be thickly covered with long grass become poor and bare. The caterpillars then pupate in the ground, to reappear later as a swarm of moths which move on, and if conditions remain suitable, devastate another place. But a toll is taken of these caterpillars by the birds that eat them, such as wattled starlings and migratory white storks and by parasitic wasps that lay their eggs in their bodies.

When it rains the clay soil in the south becomes a sticky, slippery morass which is impossible to drive over until the sun dries its surface in a pattern of cracks. It clings to the bottom of one's feet in heavy clogging masses, till it is hard work to walk. Giraffes slip and slide as they make their way to the northern parts of Nyamuluki and zebras also prefer the red soil in the rains, where the grass sprouts sweet and where their hooves are not filled with uncomfortable balls of dried mud. Cloven-hoofed animals find the clay makes hard wedges as it dries between their toes, and goats and sheep suffer if not moved to lighter soil in the rains. But the clay provides grazing for the

Spiderlings waiting on abdomen of hole-dwelling Tarantula to climb grass stems and parachute away on a breeze.

July 87

Hypolimnus misippus.

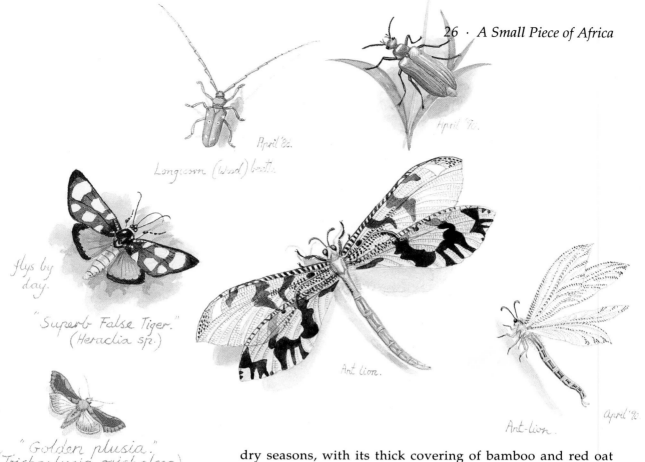

April '86.

Longicorn (Wood) beetle.

April '90.

flys by day.

"Superb False Tiger."
(Heraclia sp.)

Ant lion.

Ant-lion.

April '90.

"Golden plusia."
(Trichoplusia orichalcea).

Baby tortoise.

Tortoise's egg.
(life size)

dry seasons, with its thick covering of bamboo and red oat grasses, and it holds splendid reserves for a drought. As the rainy season progresses, the vegetation becomes thicker and heavier. The luxuriant grass cover is inhabited by a wonderful variety of crickets, beetles, grasshoppers, cicadas, moths, spiders, butterflies, bugs and aphids. Tortoises browse the succulent vegetation, mate noisily and lay their eggs. Hippoptamuses at the river lay on stocks of fat and other animals are well covered and glossy-coated. Birds bring off second broods. There are fewer flowers than earlier for many plants are setting seeds.

The rain now ends, but if it has been adequate trees continue to grow and acacia pods will ripen to provide dry-weather food for baboons, vervet monkeys and many other creatures. The grasses stay green for a while longer and prepare their beautiful and varied seedheads, but a little later a brownish tinge creeps over the land like ripeness on a plum, and the light makes pale and indigo stripes across it. The living things have reproduced and enjoyed a season of activity and plenty. Life can continue now through the coming dry season in the certainty that the rain, one day, will come again.

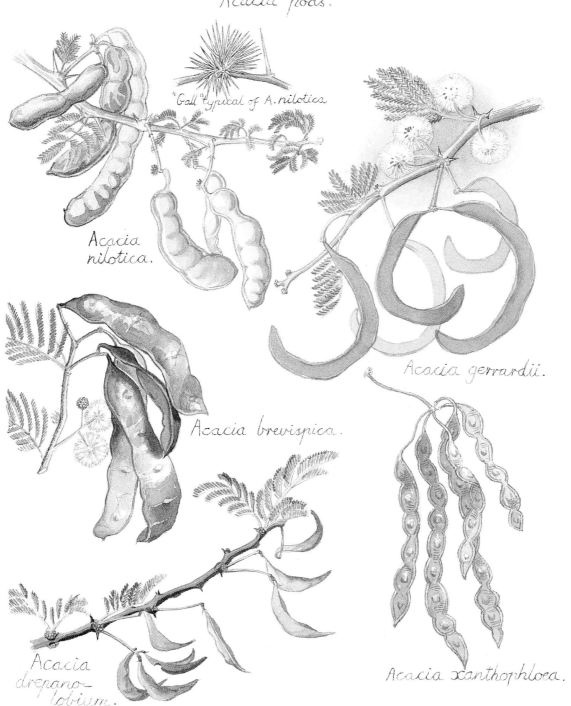

Acacia pods.

"Gall" typical of A. nilotica.

Acacia nilotica.

Acacia gerrardii.

Acacia brevispica.

Acacia drepano-lobium.

Acacia xanthophloea.

Bignoniaceae
Jacaranda mimosifolia. Jacaranda
Central and South America.

Unloading milk-
churns. Back yard.
May '91.

· **2** ·

The homestead

The homestead, with its ranch buildings, stables, dip and cattle yards, is on a rise overlooking the undulating land of Nyamuluki. To the east the eye sweeps over a series of shallow ridges and valleys to the Loldaiga Hills on the horizon. Further round to the south-east Mount Kenya lies like a dragon that is supposed to be asleep, but which keeps one eye open just a slit. To the south and south-west can be seen, though not from the house itself, the long range of the Aberdare Mountains, and to the west stretches the level horizon of the Laikipia Plateau below which, not far from the house flows the Uaso Nyiro River. To the north the land falls away into the arid that separate country highland Kenya from highland Ethiopia.

The homestead itself can be seen from afar, for it is couched beneath tall trees. Because of these trees and the presence of water, it is an oasis in the surrounding dry country, and attracts many birds that might not otherwise stay there. Black-headed orioles flute fruitily, and sling their green hammock nests. On the lawn clockwork hoopoes strut, and a pair of resident Hadada ibises often probe for beetles and spiders with their long plier beaks. Coveys of yellow-necked spurfowls and crested francolins come to scratch up clouds of dust and shout their loud tocsin of cracked bells when all is quiet in the early morning or late afternoon. A pair of paradise flycatchers build their tiny lichen and horsehair cup on a pendant twig, and as he flits under the trees, the male draws patterns in the shade with the white or chestnut streamers of his tail. Sometimes he incubates the eggs while his wife goes off to feed, and then he is ridiculously conspicuous. Of all birds, he is the Ariel or Oberon of our garden. Little purple-banded and Mariqua sun-

Amaryllidaceae

Agapanthus albiflorus.

Agapanthus. South Africa

looking N.E. from Rigalae.

2nd May 1991

The Three Hills (very rocky)

Map of Nyamuluki.
(Not to scale)

BOUNDARY LINE

E
N ← ✦ → S
W

UNEXPLORED (by author)

Rocky Ridge   High Ridge   Three Hills Plain   Tarta Gully

The Game plain   Cheetah puddle   Plain of Fire

Buffalo   cow boma   Tumble Hill

Ol Mara Dam   Toru.   Black Dam.

Ol Mara Gully.   Cheetah Corner.   Oryx Plain.   cow boma

Leopard Ridge.   Murera Dam.   The Plain of Goats.

Nyamuluki Hill.   Bat-eared Fox Plain.   Buffalo here.

Buffalo   Marera Giraffe Ridge.   Second Gully.   House Dam.   Home Plain.

Old bridge.   THE RIVER   Long Rocks   Amina Ridge   First Gully   House Dam Ridge   House Paddocks   Racire   Otter Rocks

UNKNOWN TERRITORY (to author)   Waterfall.   Papyrus Island.   Fishing Rock   Front Box   House   River Paddocks   Boathouse Bird.   THE RIVER

Twiga Crossing   Washing Rocks. The old weir.   favourite place of Elephants

Legend:
- Rocks.
- Mukiyeä woodland
- Woods or bushland with acacea trees.
- River with riverine vegetation.
- High open areas.
- Gullies with seasonal water only.
- Tracks, on black volcanic soil or red archaen soil.

birds gather excitedly in great numbers round the blossom of the jacarandas, and scarlet-chested and bronze sunbirds drink from the fluted flowers of the flame trees. At dusk, flights of green pigeons come in to roost, strangely unobtrusive. Often, one knows they are there only by their un-pigeon-like whistles and chuckles, or by their mauve-stained, coiled droppings on the ground in the morning. They are beautiful: apple-green with sapphire eyes and coral feet and beaks. Yet, in spite of this brilliant colouring, they are extremely difficult to see in the tree tops.

Another brilliant bird which is hard to see, because of the unobtrusive way in which it moves, is the sulphur-breasted bush-shrike. It can often be heard though, calling its ventriloquial 'one, two, three – four' from the garden thickets. White-browed coucals and rufous chatterers inhabit these thickets all year round, whilst squadrons of mousebirds and yellow-vented bulbuls feast on the peaches, pawpaw and lettuces of the orchard. The loud melodious song of the morning thrush, which often mimics and is mimicked by white-browed robin chats, is regularly heard. And up on our roof nests one of the sweetest singers – the African pied wagtail, or 'settlers' friend'.

At first light, speckled pigeons begin their booming, hollow calls and stamp loudly on the corrugated iron roof, contrapuntal to the tinny patter of the wagtails' feet. During the heat of the day the ring-necked doves endlessly repeated 'ka-ha-wa', and our own homing pigeons 'croodling' are as soothing as the sound of running water.

The back and sides of the house are enclosed by a kei-apple hedge, a thorny sanctuary for nesting birds and bushbabies. During the rains bees tumble and jostle with excitement among the tiny fragrant blossoms which smother it, to carry nectar and pollen away to our hives, from which we harvest honey once or twice a year. Later it bears quantities of round yellow fruits which can be made into a delicious sour jam for use with meat, or with thick cream on scones. The little brown parrots love these fruits and come from miles around to feast upon them. Sometimes the hedge is home to large black and yellow spiders which spin strong webs of orange silk among its leaves.

Small paddocks radiate from the homestead, and beyond them is the bush. In fact, the bush begins before that, for many trees and plants native to it are in the garden itself, and the same grass that grows in the paddocks and wild places comes in under the pole fences to clothe the lawn, and the same sweet wind that sweeps the bush, flows over the house and garden.

Neither the hedge nor the pole fence across the front of the garden are barriers to animals, some of whom, like the birds, are drawn by the water and plants. Many a night warthogs have rootled the lawn with their snouts and refused to be intimidated by our dogs. Porcupines come to the garden to eat the wild aloes growing there, so we sometimes have to encircle our plants with protective wire netting. How porcupines can eat these aloes I do not know, for to the human palate they are painfully, impossibly bitter. The porcupines also occasionally raid the orchard where they particularly enjoy the bark of paw-paw and mulberry trees. Recently a pair brought their young ones, marching in single file with great determination, and not to be deflected by dogs or night-watchmen, to the bucket of vegetable and fruit scraps outside the kitchen door. The parents had discovered this source of tasty titbits some nights before, and had since visited regularly, leaving discarded items strewn over the ground.

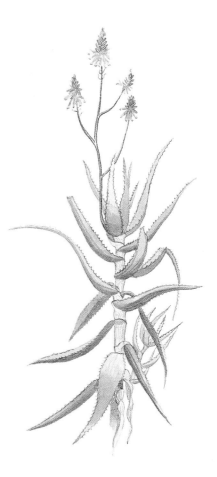

When undisturbed, porcupines glide along silently except for an occasional grunt, their black and white quills providing a wonderful camouflage in the moonlight. If frightened or annoyed they erect these impressive quills, stamp their hind feet and rattle specially adapted open-ended quills in their tails. In torchlight, their eyes glow red like rubies or hot coals.

Another visitor to the garden is the zorilla, a small skunk-like predator. My first sight of one was in November 1980, when we caught a fleeting glimpse of it disappearing behind an anthill. After that we began to see them occasionally, usually when we were returning home in the dark. Their eyes would shine in the headlights with distinctive brilliance, like rhinestones, brighter than the eyes of any other small mammal of the bush, and we would catch a glimpse of a black and white form, bottle-brush tail erect, as it scuttled out of sight. More recently zorillas have visited the garden, and outside the bedroom window one night the dogs surrounded one. Its screams were truly blood-curdling and I was frantic to help it, but as usual, could not find the torch. As we blundered about in the pitch-dark looking for it and shouting at the dogs, a strangely nauseating, though not really unpleasant, stink began to permeate the room, and the zorilla made its escape, apparently unharmed. The dogs were covered with its spray but they did not seem to mind the smell. In fact the next morning they were even rolling in the grass where the animal had been.

Shortly afterwards the dogs met another zorilla in the back yard when we were present. Screaming and squirting, it made for the garage where it 'holed up' among some planks. We went to see it after the dogs had been tied up, and it looked so menacing that we did not dare go near it.

On May 28 1989, I came upon the body of a male zorilla lying on the path leading to the mares' stable below the orchard. I think the dogs had killed him, for two of them reeked with a tell-tale stink. It measured eighteen inches from nose tip to tail tip (not counting the hair). The front paws and arms were almost bear-like, with long sharp claws. The white hair on top of its head stood up like a soft shaving brush, and the tail inside its white fur was pink and like a rat's. It was easy to see from the solidity of the body that the zorilla is related to the much larger ratel, or honey-badger. Its bravery in living near the dogs was considerable, if foolhardy.

The ratel is known for its fearless, fierce nature. It is capable of attacking anything from a buffalo to a lorry, and has been known to do both. We know they live here only from the bee

A young Zorilla (Ictonyx striatus).

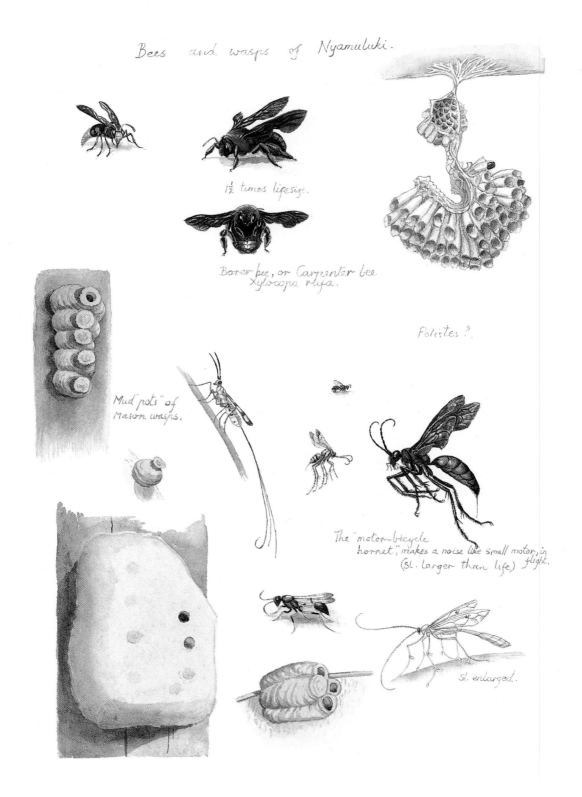

Bees and wasps of Nyamuluki.

1½ times lifesize.

Borer bee, or Carpenter bee.
Xylocopa rufa.

Polistes ?.

Mud "pots" of
Mason wasps.

The "motor-bicycle
hornet", makes a noise like small motor, in
(sl. larger than life) flight.

sl. enlarged.

hives which have been torn apart by their extremely strong jaws and claws in the process of getting out honey and grubs, of which they are very fond.

The greater honey-guide is a bird which is also fond of bee grubs and which can digest beeswax. It is said to help ratels find bees' nests and will certainly lead people to them. We have experienced this ourselves on Nyamuluki many times. A honey-guide may suddenly appear in a nearby tree, looking down at one, making its harsh repeated call. 'Oh, there you are! Follow me. Honey! Honey!' Then off it flies with purposeful mien to settle a short distance ahead. If one is not close behind, it returns at once to chatter and chastise. Then off again, a little farther this time, till eventually one is led, in a direct line, to honey. If, however, one does not choose to follow and moves off in another direction, the bird comes fussing after apparently beside itself with frustration. 'Hey! That's the wrong way. Didn't you hear? Honey! Honey!' They are always so hopeful and enthusiastic that one feels it unkind not to follow. We have sometimes been led to our own hives in this way.

Perhaps the most enchanting creature of all to visit the garden is the Senegal bush-baby. Nothing in the bush comes nearer to being a fairy or a pixie than this little animal. We once had one whom we called 'Rafiki' (Swahili for 'friend') and whom we brought into the house every evening. He progressed around the sitting room with prodigious flying leaps, having first made his hands and feet suitably sticky by urinating on them. This is a regular bush-baby habit, and probably serves to scent-mark their tree runways and advertise their presence to other bush-babies.

Rafiki would taste visitors' brandy, standing high on his long back legs and reaching down into glasses, but took no interest in whisky. The spirits did not seem to affect his jumping ability. He was very affectionate and would come onto our necks to hoot lovingly into our ears. We encouraged him to go wild, but he stayed on around the house and garden. Later we were given two other bush-babies to return to the wild, and he would visit these and hoot indignantly to see them occupying his old home – a tall cage in the bushes in a corner of the garden.

At first these newcomers were rather clumsy in the trees, particularly the male who had a number of terrifying falls; but he was so light that he came to no harm. As they became used to freedom, they objected more to being shut up in the safety of the cage when we went to bed. The little female would hold

sunbathing bees.

my finger in her teeth, very gently to begin with, but increasing the pressure steadily as my imprisoning hand approached the cage and all the time fixing my face with her huge, lambent eyes. When my hand finally reached the cage, her bite had become quite hard, though not really painful. She could not have said with more tact that she no longer wanted to be shut up. After this we left a tiny door at the top of the cage open, so that they could come and go as they wished.

A nest above the gate to my painting house is usually occupied by a female with a small baby and sometimes a juvenile as well (presumably a previous offspring). As the baby grows up there will be three large bush-babies there for a while, but when another baby is born, the oldest offspring leaves the nest. Usually I speak to them when going through the gate and sometimes they peer sleepily over the edge of the nest, soon to lose interest and snooze once more. When the weather is very hot, they sleep clinging to branches or suspended in natural hammocks of interlocking thorns and twigs so that any cooling breeze may circulate around them.

One hot afternoon I saw a pair of long legs sticking out horizontally from the nest. Their owner was obviously lying stretched on her back, tail draped comfortably over a nearby twig. When I spoke, however, the legs did not move. I tapped the branch with my paintbrushes. The legs still did not move. I began to feel that the bush-baby might be dead, so I tapped the branch really hard. The legs jerked convulsively and a little

Baby Cape geckos.

having lost tail
& grown another.

Cape gecko

with
original
tail

"Smoke-tail" or African Dormouse
(Graphiurus murinus).

head shot over the side of the nest, eyes wide with surprise
and indignation, and then beside her face appeared another,
no larger than a shilling.

Inside our house are geckoes. These small lizards live behind
pictures or in the ceilings, from which they emerge at night to
stalk insects on the walls, like miniature cats. Often before
pouncing, they wag their tails fiercely from side to side. This,
and the vertically-slit pupils of their eyes, makes their similari-
ty to cats even more striking and amusing. These house geckoes were found originally only along the coast, and are said to
have come up-country in the trunks of travelling Europeans,
perhaps as eggs, which are like tiny white ping-pong balls.

Another species of gecko, much smaller, with a black-and-
white patterned head, lives on tree branches or the woodwork
of buildings. Nearly every window or outside door of our
house has its own tenant, who guards it jealously against
poaching by fellow geckoes. It is amusing to watch one hurry
excitedly up, down and across a window pane, to catch a fly.

Attractive white-bellied mice and African dormice also live
in the ceilings of the house, and many other kinds of rats, mice
and shrews, most of which we have not managed to identify,
live around the homestead. Some of these we may have seen
only once, perhaps as corpses brought in by the cats, and it
was twenty years before we realised that spectacled elephant
shrews were living on Nyamuluki.

Grass rats frequent the farmyard and homestead and spend

Nat. size
Pygmy Mouse

Grass Rat.

Aug. 5th '90.

March 14th '88. ♂ very soft-furred, with rather Hamster-like
appearance. Nocturnal. Nat. size.
Pouched mouse.

baby White-bellied mice.

much of their day collecting grass which they carry down their holes. At certain times of year during breakfast, we can watch them bobbing out of the flower beds onto the sunburnt grass of the lawn. There they sit up to arrange blades of grass in their mouths with their hands, then back to the flower beds they bounce, hugely moustached, to disappear under the plants in puffs of dust. They are of every size, and it is endearing to see even the little 'child' rats coming out so bravely, their tails flipping merrily behind like tags of string, and the sun shining on their glossy coats.

Grass rats are food for many other creatures living nearby, including mongooses, wild cats, genets, jackals, herons, owls, marabou storks and snakes. Periodically their numbers increase to plague proportions and at such times they can consume almost all of the lucerne grown for the ranch horses. Fortunately, these plagues are short-lived, and rat numbers crash, probably through disease and starvation.

When our son Murray was four years old he found a baby white-bellied mouse crouched under the toy cupboard on the back verandah. We put her in a small basket for the night with some food, drink and a nest of hay. Next morning she was very weak and climbed onto my warm fingers as soon as I put my hand into the basket. It was clear she needed milk if she was to survive. So we made a mixture of cow's milk and water with a pinch of glucose, and she thrived on this with Farex, wheatgerm and brown bread as solid food. She would turn her tiny face to be washed with twists of warm, damp cotton-wool, her eyes screwed tight with pleasure. We gave her a nest of cotton-wool into which she would burrow and curl up in a tight little ball to sleep.

Mousey.

Stripe not always so obvious.

All day long, 'Mousey' slept, but in the evening she awoke and we took her out tobe fed, and to let her run around on the big bed. She ate a surprising amount for such a tiny creature. Sometimes she would want milk, which she lapped from the end of a pipette while clasping its glass tube with her tiny paws; at other times she showed little interest in it, or preferred to lap a drop of it from the palm of my hand.

After ten days Mousey had grown and was progressively more bouncy and electric in the evenings. We discovered that there were at least six mice of the same species living in the cupboard on the back verandah, one of whom was a mother with young at the same stage as Mousey. So we put her sleeping basket in the cupboard one evening, and half an hour later the basket was empty. Next morning she was not there, but the food that had been provided was gone. That afternoon I again

March 84.
White bellied mouse.

looked in the basket expecting it to be empty, but Mousey was there, fast asleep as usual in her cotton wool nest! That evening she played again with us on the bed, before returning to the cupboard for the night. I had seen the mother, a big mouse, squeezing through a small hole at the top of the cupboard door, so I knew they could come and go with ease. For a few weeks we continued to put food in the cupboard, and would sometimes open the door in the evening in order to watch the mice. But as Mousey was by now full grown, we could no longer distinguish her from the others. In the end they moved from the cupboard, but as we could hear them in the ceilings at night we felt sure that our mouse had made a successful return to the wild. Her descendants are still there and provide us with much pleasure and amusement.

Geckoes and mice are not the only animals to be found in the ceilings of the house and outbuildings, for there are colonies of strong-smelling free-tailed bats which fly from the eaves in fast, transparent-winged clusters at dusk, and swoop around the house squeaking and chirruping shrilly during the night. They often hunt the hundreds of small green and gold hawk-moths which hover over the spidery white blossoms of the maerua tree at the back of the house. These moths pass rapidly from flower to flower at tongue-tip distance, their fat, flexible

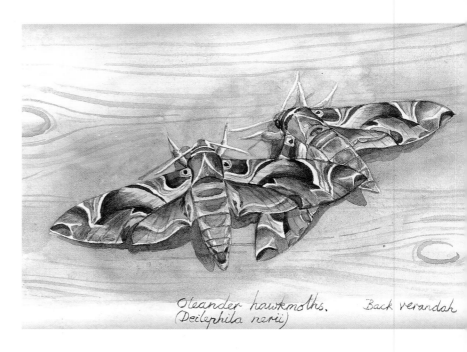

Oleander hawkmoths.   Back verandah
(Deilephila nerii)

Capparidaceae

Maerua triphylla.

Blossom much frequented
by butterflies (particularly
Pieridae) and Hawk moths.

Aug '92.

June '92.

Foliage nutricious
for small stock.

NSG

Dec. 1987. Tadarida Free-tailed bats. (*Tadarida sp.*)
Part of a large group of free-tailed bats
roosting head-down on the wall of the
petrol store. They never hang free.

At dusk they come out all together as a
flock, the late light shining through
their wings. They make various loud
squeaks audible to the human ear, &
have a strong smell. When disturbed
during the day they scuttle into hiding
behind some timbers lower down the wall.

bodies suspended between the invisible blur of their wings. Sometimes they whirr outwards in quick loops or circuits, as if impatient of the many others there. Once the bats appear, hawking round the tree like fighter-bombers zooming beneath radar detection, the moths quickly disperse. Slit-faced bats sometimes come into the house in the evenings, either down the chimney or through the windows, to catch insects attracted by the lights. During the day they roost in the garden 'long-drop'. Occasionally a yellow-bellied bat or solitary African horseshoe bat takes up temporary residence, but the easiest of all to observe is the big yellow-winged bat, for it sometimes flies and even hunts in daylight, often carrying its large baby

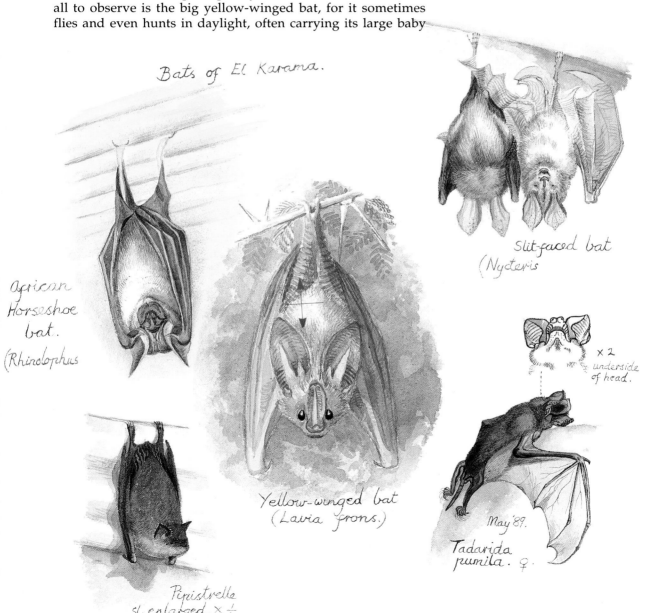

Vesper bat.
♀   (♂?)

Bats of El Karama.

Slit-faced bat
(Nycteris

African
Horseshoe
bat.
(Rhinolophus

× 2
underside
of head.

Yellow-winged bat
(Lavia frons.)

May '89.
Tadarida
pumila. ♀.

Pipistrelle
sl. enlarged. × ¼

Bats leaving roof

clinging to its underside. These bats have special trees in which they may roost for many years. One such tree in the First Gully was occupied by a pair of yellow-wings continuously for over fifteen years. Perhaps they were the same individuals, for bats can be surprisingly long-lived.

Not all the animals around the homestead are small. On March 10 1977, I wrote in my notebook:

> Yesterday Laria, Bella and I had a wonderful experience with a wild bull giraffe when we were filling the square trough in the top of the River Paddock. The giraffe was feeding on a tree nearby taking no notice of our voices. After a while he walked right up to us and was lowering his head very gently to sniff the children, when I stepped forward anxiously, and he turned and walked slowly away to the nearest tree where he began again to browse. This seemed all the more wonderful because I had given this same giraffe a fright a quarter of an hour earlier, when I had crept up to the mukuriundu tree upon which he had been feeding, and taken a photograph of his legs and tummy through the branches. We had met at the side of the tree and he had shied away.

This was 'Roman Nose', whom I had first seen when I came to live on Nyamuluki. Then, he was a stripling of thirteen feet or so in height. Gradually, over the years he increased in size until he was a large bull some eighteen feet tall. He had grown used to everyone who lived around the homestead and, after the above incident, showed no fear except of strangers, whom he recognised as such instantly and regarded with suspicion. He would walk through gates which we held open for him, though he could easily step over them, and browse unconcernedly near working men. Once I offered him salt from my hand, but as he lowered his head I lost my nerve. What if he began to follow us around asking for salt? It would be unnerving and possibly dangerous to have such a gigantic follower, so I desisted. But he used to help himself with relish from the salt boxes put out for the cattle.

Roman Nose was always to be seen around the house and paddocks, except for the times when he went off into the bush, presumably to look for interesting females. Sometimes he would be away for months, but he always came back. His last absence, which occurred when he must have been well over twenty years old, was a long one, and we thought he would not return. But he did. He was ill and thin, with a wound

Solanaceae.

Solanum
incanum

Solanum
species A?

Solanum
mauense.

Solanum
nigrum.

Solanum
terminale.

Ears normally folded back along top edge & hanging like a curtain.

from life sketches (Not to scale with each other) showing different colours according to colour of earth they have "dusted" with; and typical positions.

Done while looking through binoculars at elephants on other side of the River

behind his off front leg, and he stood listlessly without feeding. I offered him salt from a *karai* (a shallow metal basin) which I held up as high as I could reach, but he was too weak to take any interest in it. After a few days he disappeared. Many weeks later we found his remains in a thicket near the river, not far from his old haunts, where he had gone to die in peace soon after we last saw him alive.

Fighting Giraffes.

Roman Nose has been replaced now, as house giraffe, by another big bull whom we call, perhaps unfairly, 'Meat Paste', owing to the light pinkish colour of his markings. The giraffes of Nyamuluki, though they are supposed to be the reticulated race, vary greatly in colour. Some bulls are so darkly marked that one would describe their colour as maroon, or even black. Many are the more typical chestnut or liver-chestnut and white, some having widely spaced squares of colour on the white background, while the markings of others are thinly separated by a fine reticulation. They seem to be an amalgam of three subspecies of giraffe, not quite typical of any; in colour sometimes like the Nubian, and in form similar to the Rothchild's, the bulls often having extra pairs of small 'horns' behind the large front ones.

From the back yard we can see the far side of the river valley – steep, curved and forested with acacia and mukinyea. Along the valley bottom tall yellow-thorns mark the line of the river. Above and beyond the valley stretches a sea-like horizon, pale gold and azure in the morning, indigo-striped at midday, insubstantial in a haze of gold or amethyst in the evening, and hard and black against the star-filled sky at night. Elephants move up and down this valley. Sometimes we see more than two hundred of them, progressing with the slow, majestic momentum of huge boulders carried on a lava flow. Often at night they come up to the yards and buildings to taste the pepper trees, of which they are very fond and sometimes they lean over the orchard hedge to remove a few banana trees. After eating the trunks and foliage, they leave the bunches of bananas untouched on the ground, for presumably they do not enjoy these unless they are ripe. Once, three elephants lifted the narrow gate from its wooden pintles, and walked single file through the orchard trees, sampling oranges and *sukuma wiki* (a kind of kale). On hearing the night-watchman approach, they turned back carefully without breaking anything and stole silently away, leaving a telltale scent of chewed oranges on the still night air.

Nakurundu tree

They have also learned to slide the poles of a pole gate, in order to enter the back yard undetected, though at other times they may break the fences with loud snaps and seem not to care who knows of their coming. Then the night-watchmen beat old tins and blow whistles to frighten them away.

On the whole elephants are peaceful. If seriously disturbed they can, of course, be dangerous and destructive, and at least eight people have been killed by them in the neighbourhood during recent years.

If elephants are a potential danger round the homestead, some snakes are another, for various kinds, both venomous and harmless, are not uncommon. We see them only occasionally as they are normally shy and retiring. The most common, perhaps, are the beautiful little spotted bush snakes, thin as whip-cord and emerald green, with large gold-rimmed eyes, or the bold olive grass snakes which live in the garden and feed on toads, birds and mice. Boomslangs have sometimes taken up residence in the kei-apple hedge, and centipede-eaters, white-lipped or herald snakes, brown house snakes and some unidentified types are also seen from time to time. All snakes

Puff-adder (*Bitis arietans*) ♀.
January 20th 1988 in garden.
Asymmetrically marked on rear half

Reptiles.

in Kei-apple hedge   Sept '71.

Head of female Boomslang.
(*Dispholidus typus*)

A baby Herald, or
White-lipped snake.
Feb '87. (*Crotaphopeltis
hatamboeia*)

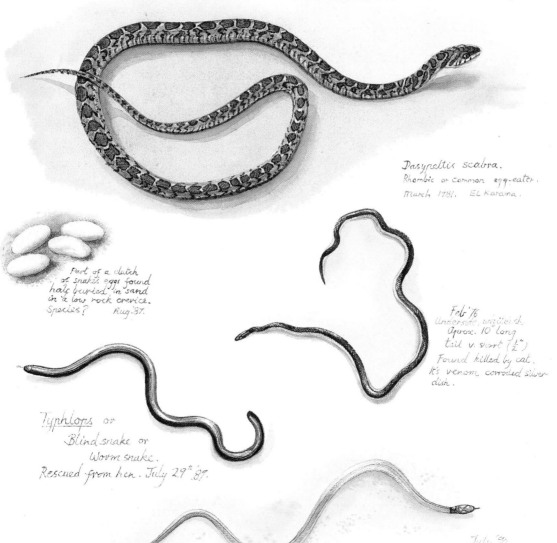

Dasypeltis scabra.
Rhombic or common egg-eater.
March 1981. El Katana.

Part of a clutch
of snake's eggs found
half buried in sand
in a low rock crevice.
Species?   Aug '87.

Feb '76
Underside, whitish.
Aprox. 10" long
tail v. short (½")
Found killed by cat.
It's venom corroded silver
dish.

Typhlops or
Blind snake or
Worm snake.
Rescued from hen. July 29ᵗʰ '87.

July '93.
Cape Centipede-eater or
Black-headed Snake (*Aparallactus capensis*)
found Amana Ridge.

Chameleon.
Sept 78.

are beautiful, even the sinister Aztec-plumaged puff-adder with its stony eye, who swallows hares whole and gives birth to live young instead of laying eggs. The puff-adders are perhaps the most dangerous of all the snakes that live on Nyamuluki because they rely on their wonderful camouflage to keep them hidden, and do not bother to move out of the way when one approaches.

When our younger daughter was about four years old, I noticed her pulling out a small chest on the back verandah behind which, the day before, she had arranged a 'garden' of pieces of orange and lemon peel. The box was not heavy, but some God-sent impulse made me go to help her, though I was busy at the time. Behind the chest had fallen a flattened inflatable goose. As I bent to pick it up, and little Isabella had already started to push behind the box, I noticed a scaly loop protruding from beneath the goose. A puff-adder had curled up there in the midst of the orange and lemon peel garden, thinking it had found a quiet place in which to hide.

We have found puff-adders in the garden many times. Once, a mixed bird party's noisy scolding and I went to discover the cause. Arriving at where they were gathered, I saw only dead leaves on the ground. Stirring them with stick, I at once felt the heavy, muscular body of a puff-adder that was concealed under a thin layer of the leaves. Even when not so covered, they are sometimes extraordinarily difficult to see.

The other dangerous snake of Nyamuluki is the black-necked spitting cobra, but though it can be a large, active reptile it prefers to avoid man, and may live for many years in its own territory nearby without being noticed. For self-defence these cobras can spit their venom accurately at an enemy's eyes from a distance of several yards. Fortunately they seldom bite, which may be fatal to the recipient.

One evening, Isabella, then six years old, slipped out of the bedroom door to talk to the old black cat, Bhageera. She heard a rustling, or 'puffing' as she later described it (this was the thrusting of dry scales against the paving), and saw a dark shape seeming to undulate towards her below the sitting-room window. At first she thought it was a long piece of cloth blowing in the wind – but there was no wind. She backed hastily into the doorway and called 'Mum, I think there's a snake … yes, it *is* a snake, and it's coming in here!' I pulled her inside and shut the door quickly. We went to the window and shining a torch through it, saw a large cobra coiled against the door. Guy climbed out of the sitting-room window with his gun, while I held the torch to illuminate the snake. It was as

a young spitting-cobra.

well that no second shot was needed, for at the first the torch beam leapt wildly and took some time to refocus. Not only was the unfortunate snake's head shattered, but there was a hole in the bottom of the door which is there to this day. Bhageera, normally a brave cat, was nervous for some days afterwards. He would look carefully behind doors before going through them, and if something touched him unexpectedly he would jump out of his skin.

We kill only those cobras which are seen in or near the house or stables, or near the stock *bomas* (small circular enclosures, usually made of cut brush), though any snake capable of killing a rat is a valuable ally, especially when the rodent populations reach plague proportions. Perhaps it is the availability of rodents and toads around the homestead that attracts the snakes.

Leopard toads, which live in and around the garden, spend the dry season in damp flower pots, holes in trees, under stones or inside old boots. They let us know when rain is imminent by starting to croak sleepily from these retreats, and as the rains draw nearer, they croak more often and louder. At this time two optimistic males take up position in the small concrete duck pond by the dairy, and start a deafening duet of croaking in the evenings. They keep this up late into the night. One is a baritone and the other a bass, and their croaks are alternated carefully. As soon as there is an accidental synchronisation, they immediately readjust to alternate: 'Quack-kwark, quack-kwark, quack-kwark!' with the metallic ratcheting sound of a fishing reel. Sometimes the noise is so loud and monotonous that the night-watchman is instructed to shine his torch on them at intervals, which silences them for a minute or two. Sometimes they break off for a wrestling match, but once one has managed to hold the other, protesting, under the surface for a few seconds, they retire to their own corners to start their duet once more. What the female toads think of these two one can only guess, but we seldom see any visit them, perhaps because the pond is unsuitable for their long chaplets of eggs as it is regularly drained and cleaned, and the ducks swim in it all day long.

As the rains progress, toads seem to be everywhere and often make their way into the house, where we find them in all sorts of unexpected places. One night, on awaking thirsty and reaching sleepily for my bedside glass, I got no drink. Tilting it higher, and finally upending it over my face, a trickle of indescribably horrible-tasting liquid entered my mouth. Spluttering and by now fully awake, I reached for the torch. There was a

♂ (v. sl. lgr than life)

June 1990.

Walker's Owl (Erebus macrops.)
family Noctuidae.

-15ᵗʰ May 1991
A rather worn individe
Arrow Sphinx (Lophosteth

fat toad wedged comfortably in the glass, from which it had displaced most of the water and fouled what remained. I could not help bursting into horrified laughter.

Toads seem to like the cool, polished concrete floors in the house, and they also come to catch some of the many insects that are attracted to the lamps in the evenings. Geckoes and spiders also take advantage of the lamps to catch insects, but the praying mantis, known to everyone as the implacable huntress who will even eat her own mate alive, is strangely inoffensive when drawn to the light at night. I have seldom seen one take advantage of the situation to seize prey, and it seems rather odd (if an insect is purely instinctive) that it does not react automatically to the stimulus of prey blundering into its special insect-catching front legs.

Exciting species of moths quite often come to the lamps, and some of them are obliging enough to stay peacefully on the paper or on my hand while I paint them. Other insects may have to be stalked patiently with much creeping and crawling. I also take advantage of the occasional corpses that we find, though the colours of living insects are much richer and more beautiful than of those that have been dead for a while, and much of their character, of course, is in the way they move and hold themselves. Sometimes good opportunities to paint are missed for one reason or another. Once on a walk we came upon an exciting vermilion caterpillar, but although I had started out with a pencil it had been dropped somewhere along the way. The big caterpillar was too frisky to bring home on a piece of vegetation, and none of us had a handkerchief in which to imprison it. I have been hoping ever since to meet another such caterpillar, but it was the only one of its kind any of us have seen.

One could go on painting different insects for ever, for there are literally countless kinds, with their relatives the spiders, millipedes, centipedes and others, living in the bush of Nyamuluki, in an incredible variety of colours and forms. Some, of such small size that they can be seen properly only with a magnifying glass, are yet of marvellous beauty. It is a wonder how each manages to find its mate among such a bewildering diversity of species. In the rainy season, one has only to see the almost frightening number of different kinds of small moths gathered at an outside light, to feel the same sense of wonder and bewilderment that a sky full of infinitely distant stars creates.

Some insects such as bees and disease-carrying mosquitoes together with ticks and a few spiders might be called dangerous (we have not yet seen a scorpion on Nyamuluki). Among them are the siafu or safari ants. They were quite common until the drought of 1981 when they died off, and even now in 1993 they have not fully recovered. Before this, they would often appear in sinister, solid red streams an inch or two wide, which would flow over the ground, splitting into secondary streams here, plaiting and rejoining there, but always searching for living prey. Other insects and arthropods were overpowered and eaten on the spot or carried along as spoil; lizards, geckoes, caterpillars, small snakes and nestlings were engulfed. Anything injured, or for some reason unable to get out of the way, was eaten alive. Often we would have to spread lines of hot ash and coals around the chicken houses and even around our own house. If they had got into the hen houses the poultry would have been killed. Dogs in kennels, ponies in stables, babies in cots – nothing was safe unless it was free to escape or call for help.

One night our bedroom was invaded, and by the time we awoke the siafu had entered the small side room where our baby Laria was asleep. Moving ropes of them braided the floor and walls, and I had to pick my way via the few uncovered

An assassin-bug

sl. lgr. than life
Ground beetles

sl. lgr. than life.

A Ground beetle.

wood beetle.

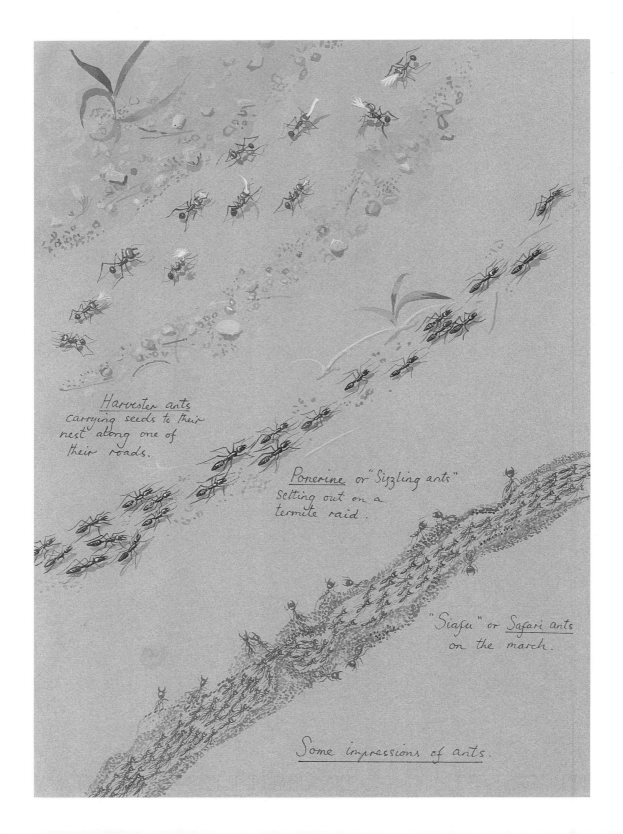

Harvester ants carrying seeds to their nest along one of their roads.

Ponerine or "Sizzling ants" setting out on a termite raid.

"Siafu" or Safari ants on the march.

Some impressions of ants.

islands on the floor to the side of the cot, remove the net, and carry Laria back to our bed. Meanwhile hot coals were brought, and with the aid of these and pyrethrum, the siafu were overpowered.

Siafu are nomadic within large territories and make temporary homes in hollows underground or in sheltered spots beneath thickets. There they gather into great seething balls, their queens somewhere safe inside, the outsides bristling with the world's fiercest soldiery. We once watched a solid column of them coming out of a hole and disappearing into another a few inches on. This column, an inch wide, continued to flow solidly for three days and three nights. It might be suggested that they were going round in a circle underground, and we have indeed seen siafu circling accidentally. However, they have always realigned after a few minutes, and managed to break the circle.

We began to get to know insects, and to feel that each one was an aware individual, when we had to hunt for them in order to raise a succession of wild bird chicks to adulthood. I very much disliked this catching of insects, but we had to be ruthless in order to keep our fledgelings alive.

One of these was found by Laria under the pepper tree outside the back verandah. Its nest had fallen to the ground in a storm, and the other chick in it was dead. Cheepie was a Speke's weaver and was not far from being fully fledged when found, which I am sure was to her advantage. At first, as so often happens with wild birds, we had to forcibly open her beak to feed her; but after a very short while she was gaping eagerly every time the cover was taken from her box. To begin with we fed her on small pieces of meat dipped in wheatgerm, which we soon supplemented with any insects we managed to catch. She began to fly to us whenever we entered the room, and would shake her wings so vigorously when begging for food, that her face became a blurr and the slipstream under her wings felt strong and cool.

A few days later, when she had become quite strong at flying, we took her outside on my shoulder and perched her in the maerua tree outside the back verandah for an hour or two every morning. With a little coaxing she would come near enough to be fed by tweezers, or would fly to my hand. We would take her inside again for the afternoon and night, and at this stage she left her box and began to roost in a basket on a high ledge that she had discovered.

After a few days of this routine we began to leave her outside all day, and she would fly down to our heads or shoulders whenever we appeared. Early on we learnt to recognise her call and could distinguish it instantly from those of the many other weaver chicks that were calling almost deafeningly from the surrounding trees. We still took her inside for the night, and first thing in the morning would feed her on moths we had caught at the lamps the evening before, supplemented with meat. Next, we removed a pane of glass from a window so that she could come and go as she wished, and she began to accompany us as we searched for insects to feed her. She would perch on us or hop on the ground in front of us, watching. We were not very good at finding insects at first but we quickly improved. To begin with Cheepie seemed to have no idea what we were doing. She did not try to catch insects herself even if one was in front of her 'nose', and she ate only that which was put directly into her beak. In this way a weaver must learn from its mother what is good to eat, and what is not, for it does not seem to know by instinct. Unfortunately, we did not always know either, and after feeding her an extremely distasteful (perhaps even poisonous) butterfly, she refused from then on to eat any butterflies, even types that she had previously enjoyed.

After two weeks had elapsed, Cheepie began to pick up insects from the palm of my hand, and then to catch them herself. But even so she would not try anything she had not eaten before, unless it was presented to her. She would sit on my finger like a miniature trained falcon as we walked through the grass, peering downwards. If I saw an insect I would put my hand near it and Cheepie would dive for it without letting go of my finger, so that often she was hanging upside-down from it with an insect firmly grasped in her beak. If she saw something I had missed, she flew down for it immediately, afterwards returning to my hand. She loved these hunts and would drive me out on them by cheeping loudly into my ear. But once the hunt had begun she became very quiet, until she caught something, when she would cheep cheerfully after swallowing it. If I caught something she would cheep before swallowing it, as if to say thank you. The amount she could eat, and the size of the insects she could swallow never ceased to fill us with amazement. Flying must use a tremendous amount of energy.

Later Cheepie enjoyed accompanying us on walks, often as far as the First Gully a quarter of a mile away, or to the cottage where I had been painting window frames. She would fly alongside from bush to bush, or go on ahead and come back to us when she felt like it. If dusk approached while we were out she would become increasingly restless, flying off, circling

Sketches of "Cheepy" (a Speke's weaver).

The approach......

Coming in to land on my head.

Inspecting a distasteful insect.

round and returning until finally she would set off in a direct line for the house, her little figure growing smaller and smaller with distance, her cheep sounding fainter and fainter, until she disappeared into the big trees of the garden.

After about a week of sleeping in her basket, Cheepie decided to move to an abandoned weaver's nest hanging with others from the pepper tree over the back verandah. Later, she changed her nest once or twice, but always went to roost in one before dark. Sometimes we went out in the car and did not return till after dark, when we would call her name under the nests, and at once she would answer with her own sleepy little chirp. Sometimes she poked her head out, but nothing would induce her to leave her nest after nightfall.

Early in the morning we would hear her calling outside the bedroom window, and as soon as I went out, she came whizzing down with many a side-slip and spiral from the top of the big jacaranda tree on the lawn. I had a small dish of meat ready on the early-morning tea-tray for her breakfast. When hungry she had a disconcerting habit of flying at my nose (beak?), though later she learned that this was not approved of.

After a month she began to go to our favourite hunting grounds by herself, and became less demanding; we also noticed her eating grass seeds, which must have helped to blunt the edge of her appetite. Later, as an adult, she would feed mainly on seeds and vegetable matter.

Cheepie bathed at least once every day. If she heard us washing our hands in the basin, she would fly merrily in through the window and have her bath under the tap; otherwise she would bathe under the garden hose-pipe when I watered the flowers in the afternoon. She could be maddening, as when she sat on my shoulder and cheeped loudly and incessantly into my ear. This usually happened when I was having difficulties with the children, or at some other demanding moment. She had no fear of dogs, and often settled on their backs – a highly dangerous activity, though the cats were a greater anxiety. She had, however, an instant and instinctive reaction to hawks, taking cover and remaining quiet as the local black Gabar goshawk or his ordinary grey mate came into the garden.

Cheepie would come to tea with us and attack the loaf with gusto, or land on the muslin cover of the milk jug which would slowly subside till her toes touched the milk, when she would scramble out again. Sometimes she did something much worse to the milk so that it had to be given to the cats.

In July, during her second month with us, Cheepie began to

Momordica
foetida.

Zehneria
scabra.

♀ flower.

Lagenaria
abyssinica.

Cucurbitaceae.

Compositae.

Osteospermun

Senecio
discifolius.

Bidens

Gutenbergia

spend longer periods away, and, as the other Speke's weavers were still in the trees outside the verandah, she spent more time with them, flying happily about the farmyard with a flock of females and immatures.

Suddenly, one day, all the weavers disappeared – gone on one of their mysterious visits to a different part of the country. We never knew where they went, or why, but go they did – and they took Cheepie with them.

It was three months before we saw Cheepie again. Then, one morning, we all heard her unmistakeable call in the maerua tree. We hurried out of the house and I coaxed her down to eat some wheat held in the palm of my hand. She came hesitantly, took a few grains, then flew off to join the other weavers who had reappeared as suddenly as they had left. Cheepie had returned to her own kind, and having politely bid us goodbye, we lost touch. As a weaver matures it stops using its baby call, so we could no longer recognise her voice.

It always rather surprises me that there should be so much 'rapport' between birds and humans, when our common origins separated so far back, but there seems to be. We will always enjoy the memory of Cheepie's vivid, cheerful personality and those of the other weavers we raised, and be thankful for what she taught us of bird character and behaviour. Being a bird mother (along with being a human one) though very demanding, has been one of my loveliest experiences.

A pair of Ethiopian swallows have lived in the house with us for nine years. Each year they have raised two broods in their nest in the corner of the sitting-room, and the cock has filled the house with his most musical song. After breeding, the parent birds sometimes, though not always, continue to roost in the house throughout the rest of the year. They show remarkable adaptability and intelligence in finding their way in and out of different doors and windows, and the whole house would be full of swallowsand their nests if we allowed all our prospective lodgers in. The stables and garage are already full of breeding pairs, for buildings make good substitutes for the caves which they traditionally use.

During the third year of their residence in the sitting-room while they were raising the first brood of the season, our cock bird lost his mate to one of our cats. But in spite of the fact that the young were still small enough to need brooding (which cock swallows do not do) he managed successfully to raise three chicks by himself. For the first four days after the mother's death I attempted at intervals to 'brood' them with a small bottle filled with hot water and wrapped in cotton-wool.

Ethiopian swallows roosting by their nest in a stable

We even made a tiny quilt of muslin stuffed with goose down, but the young always knocked this off even when we tied it on with cotton. Next year our swallow had found a new mate and they have been together ever since. They are not at all concerned about lights in the evening, or even dinner parties. When they have young, they often continue in the artificially extended daylight to catch flies from the ceiling.

In the garden, sunbirds build small hanging nests of tiny twigs, grasses, lichen and spiders' webs. These have round entrances in the sides, with projecting verandahs over them to keep out the sun and the rain. Recently a pair of bronze sunbirds had trouble with their nest, which hung from a low twig of the big jacaranda. It began when storms caused a nearby twig to wear a gaping hole in the back of the nest, which we discovered when we found the chick cheeping on the ground.

We patched the hole with a flat wad of cotton-wool held in place with Sellotape. The chick was replaced and its parents continued to feed it as if nothing had happened. Then the whole nest fell to the ground. We sewed it back onto the twig with wool, but a few days later it was obviously about to fall again. This time we strapped it firmly in place with bands of black insulating tape wound round the whole nest lengthways. The parents carried on looking after their chick unconcernedly in this, by now, very queer looking patched nest. They had been interested spectators of all these measures on their behalf, and their relaxed behaviour made us think that they understood what we were doing, or, that they knew us very well. Soon afterwards, the chick flew successfully.

In contrast was the behaviour of another pair of the same species which showed little of this kind of sense. We found the nest on the ground with a little black chick inside it, but not knowing exactly where in the tree it had been, we had to guess. We must have guessed wrong, for though the chick called for food and the parents were frantic to feed it, they would not go near the nest, and we think the chick may have died. This seemed strange, for once a bronze sunbird chick

Young Ethiopian swallows nearly ready to fly. May.

nest of
Jackson's
Widow-bird.

leaves its nest, the parents will continue to feed it wherever it is, simply by responding to its call. Perhaps these were inexperienced parents, or maybe the position of the nest was crucial in some way at that particular time. On the other hand, they may have continued to feed it when quite sure they were unwatched, for in observing nature it is very easy to jump to wrong conclusions or be misled, unless one is prepared to take great pains.

The way nests are built is intriguing. The purple grenadier surrounds the outer walls of its ball-shaped nest with the featheriest of grass heads, so that the whole thing appears insubstantial, almost smokey, and could easily be mistaken for a mass of spider's web. I once found one of these nests lined with tufts of Guy's hair, which must have been collected off the lawn after a hair-cutting session. It had been carried at least five hundred yards and must have taken the birds several journeys to transport.

After a pair of fire-finches had flown and were living away from their spherical nest, I took it down and pulled it to pieces to see how it was made. We were surprised at the size of some of the twigs, grasses and feathers that had been woven into its walls. The fire-finch is a tiny bird, like an animated plum, and we have watched them being blown off course when carrying even quite small feathers of the type used for lining the nest. But here were chicken's wing feathers five or six times the length of the little bird itself, and heavy stems of grass much longer than those. The nest chamber was thickly lined all round – floor, ceiling and walls – with the curved breast feathers of other birds. It was wonderfully soft and warm, but had not been kept very clean, for it was full of dried droppings. Small ants had made their nest in its lower storeys.

Striped swallows often have bad luck with their nests at the homestead, for they build them on the undersides of verandah ceilings, or on corrugated iron which contracts and expands with heat, so that the heavy, flask-shaped mud structures often crash to the ground, sometimes when eggs have already been laid. When they build from a stable base they are more successful, but even then they are not safe, for piratical white-rumped swifts often forcibly take over their nests, afterwards reinforcing them with their own glue mixture. Little swifts build for themselves and there is a colony of spit-and-feather nests under the corrugated iron porch outside the ranch office. How their young survive the temperature inside these nests at midday is a mystery. They really are as hot as ovens, as we discovered when returning fallen chicks to their homes.

Didric cuckoo

Ethiopian swallow

Spekes weaver

White rumped swift

Crowned plover

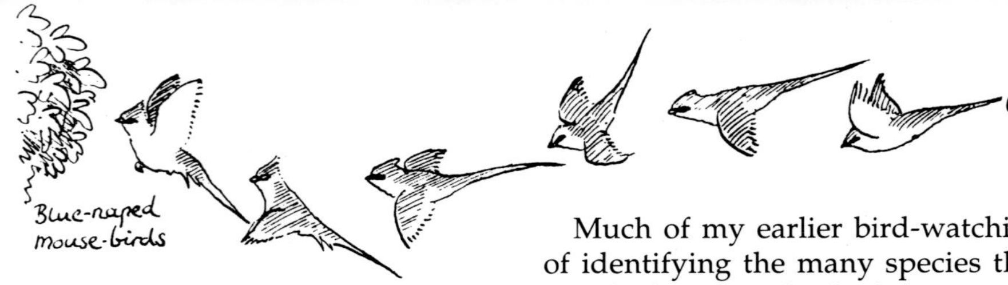

Blue-naped
mouse-birds

Much of my earlier bird-watching on Nyamuluki consisted of identifying the many species that I had never seen before: nearly four hundred of them; and that of course was very exciting. As the years went by it became harder to add new birds to the list though there are still rarities which appear now and again to thrill us. But once most of the birds had been identified, I started to concentrate on the far greater pleasure of watching them going about their daily lives – intricate lives enjoyed quite independently of humans and their concerns, and of great beauty and sweetness. Sometimes I see things that have perhaps never been seen before, and others that people would question, or that are puzzling. But the thing that gives us most pleasure about birds is not the possible discovery of new scientific facts, or even of a new species, but the way in which they carry on their lives all around us. They are so confident and busy, so unconsciously obedient to the laws that have been laid down for them, yet utterly free; each one is so bursting with vitality that we earth-bound mammals seem slow and plodding beside them.

Nest of
Chinspot flycatcher

April 24ᵉ '90.
At base of grass tuft.
2ⁿᵈ gully N. of Housedam.

LJG

Acacia nilotica.

Blue-naped Mousebird
(Urocolius macrourus)

Liliaceae.

Gloriosa simplex.

NJG

· **3** ·

The Paddocks

The paddocks which surround the homestead, and through which we so often walk, are simply areas of natural bush and grassland that have been enclosed by fences. In them we keep stock which for some reason needs to be near headquarters instead of out in the bush with the flocks and herds.

Perhaps the most interesting paddocks are those that border on the river, for they are full of thickets in which *Carissa edulis* bears its clusters of pink and white jasmine-scented flowers, and where the flames of gloriosa lilies flicker. Here too the tiny round leaves of *Phyllanthus* shade the duiker's secret couches, and beneath the *Rhus* bowers of branches, give browse to steinbuck. There are rocky places with their own interesting flora, and numerous winding game paths along which we may meet bushbuck and waterbuck. The tall and shaggy-coated waterbuck is one of my favourite antelopes; when alarmed it has a wonderful way of trotting, exaggerated and syncopated, each foot lifted high with a flying pause between strides, like certain movements of a High School horse. It is a bewitching sight to see a mother waterbuck followed by her baby, both trotting in this slow motion way.

There are usually fresh or dried elephant droppings in the

1   2   3   4   5

Waterbuck (Defassa)
Kobus defassa.

Anacardiaceae.

Rhus natalensis.

Edible fruit
enjoyed by children
and baboons. Ascorbic-
acid flavour.

Aug '72.

River Paddocks, and the splattered chaff-filled dung and four-toed tracks of hippopotamuses. At night hippos sometimes come right up to the farmyard fence to eat the short grass there, which for some reason they seem particularly to enjoy. In the hippo breeding season we hear their hollow hoots and bellows, and once I saw a pair mating in the deep, slow water at the first bend of the river, not far from the yards. In wet weather they may come out to graze in the paddocks during the day, moving their ponderous bulk with an airy lightness, seeming almost to float, as they scythe the grass from side to side. We have to be careful not to run into them, for they can be very dangerous.

Hippo track.

There is always the possibility of meeting elephants in the River Paddocks, and recently the children came face to face with a very large bull elephant there. They were on their way down to the river to cut bamboos to make into musical pipes and had just reached the corner of a tall kei-apple hedge round an old enclosure, when Murray saw the way blocked by a rusty wall. 'Elephant!' he exclaimed, and shot off at top speed in the opposite direction, closely followed by the others. He said afterwards that its head seemed to reach the sky, and its tusks the ground. They think that the elephant never saw them, and indeed elephants are very short-sighted. They have as a result of this myopia a strange, inward-turned, somnambulant expression on their faces, rather lovely and mysterious to behold.

Sometimes at night we hear elephants pass through the river paddocks, like a hurricane without wind. Trees and branches crack loudly as they are broken, and swish as they fall, while the terrific screams and blasting trumpets of the elephants themselves send a thrill up one's spine. One can see how, in the past, elephants played a vital role as they wandered over the vast landscape, knocking down and uprooting trees to keep areas of grassland open and thus increasing the number of habitats available for other animals. In some of the tangles of knocked-down branches other trees could germinate and grow protected, ensuring a constant rotation of grass and bush. In drought, elephants excavate many holes in the beds of sand-rivers, providing a water supply for the animals that cannot dig.

Predators may occur anywhere on Nyamuluki, and they are often seen in the paddocks. Of them, one of the most interesting is the Cape hunting dog, the round-eared, harlequin-coated wild dog of Africa. These dogs seem to say, as they stare at you with their unwinking yellow eyes, that you are their equal and worthy of their curiosity. People normally find dogs attractive, and they seem to reciprocate the feeling; perhaps because they smile as we do, and have greeting ceremonies. Also their feet smell similar to ours, which may have something to do with the friendship – at least on one side! Yet hunting dogs are often hated because of the way they tear their living prey to pieces (though the much loved domestic dogs will do just the same when in a pack), or for the implacable determination with which they follow and usually kill an animal that they single out from a herd. Yet surely their high rate of success is a result of stamina and a cooperative method of hunting? Other animals do seem to be very afraid of them when they are hunting.

Mantis.

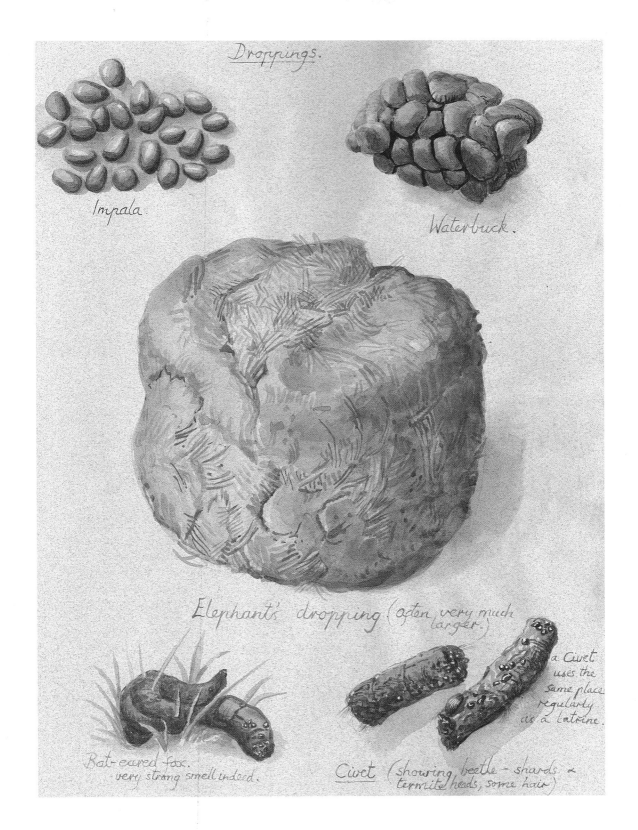

Droppings.

Impala.

Waterbuck.

Elephant's dropping (often very much larger.)

Bat-eared fox. very strong smell indeed.

Civet (showing beetle-shards & termite heads, some hair)

a Civet uses the same place regularly as a latrine.

African Hunting dogs, on Toru.

I remember a herd of impala rushing in amongst some piles of cut brush that we were burning, when a pack of thirteen hunting dogs appeared not far off. It seemed that their fear of the dogs had quite outweighed their usual fear of men and fire; or perhaps they were so distracted that they did not notice where they were going. On another occasion, when Guy was walking through one of the paddocks, an impala buck rushed past him and straight into a fence breaking its neck instantly. The buck was closely followed by a pack of hunting dogs. Guy shouted to frighten them off, as they were milling round excitedly. They withdrew reluctantly, and the impala's body was brought home where it provided some welcome venison (an impala buck weighs about a hundred and fifty pounds).

In the 1970s large packs of hunting dogs were still met with and they occasionally harassed our flocks of sheep and goats. On the morning of November 17 1973, one of our herdsmen arrived in the back yard in a state of excitement with his whole flock, swearing that he had been surrounded by a pack of fifty dogs. Even allowing for exaggeration, it must have been a big pack to have produced such an effect on him. More often we saw them in groups of six to ten. Though they have seldom bothered stock on Nyamuluki because there was so much game around, on other ranches where there was little or no game, or flocks were left unattended, they have caused havoc, particularly among sheep. Perhaps this is another reason for their unpopularity.

Tragically, the diseases of domestic dogs, and rabies, have so decimated the hunting dog that now it is in danger of extinction. In 1986 they reappeared here for the first time since the bad outbreak of rabies in early 1982. In 1988 a pack of twenty were seen; in 1989 only eight, and we have not yet seen them since. With ever increasing human pressure on the land and a consequent increase in domestic dogs and decrease in natural prey, it will be harder for the African wild dog to survive. We would not dream, nowadays, of appropriating a kill of theirs for they need all the help they can get.

Whilst pushing a pram through the paddocks and bush when the children were babies, I was always more anxious at the thought of meeting a territorial cock ostrich than a lion. I naturally avoided the sort of areas where we might possibly meet lions, and kept to the more open country of the kind frequented by ostriches, where it was easier to push the pram. Not that we have ever been threatened by an ostrich, but we had heard stories of people being disembowelled by their kicks, or chased and knocked off bicycles, and I thought they might mistake the black and white pram for a rival bird. Once a cock ostrich did run after a small Piper Cub aircraft we were in, to be left dancing in earth-bound impotence, neck and thighs red with emotion and breeding season fervour, as we took off.

The lions of Nyamuluki usually go about their own lives unseen, being much more wary than their National Park relatives. However, we have all met them when out walking or driving in vehicles. Guy once came upon a lion and lioness feeding on an adult giraffe that they had killed in a small paddock in front of the house. They growled at him as he withdrew. Later, the children and I had fun making casts of their tracks with Polyfilla. You could see where the lioness had

Sahiwal cow.

made her final stalk and rush, with her outspread claws digging deeply into the earth.

One evening when I was returning to the house after a solitary walk, I heard above the buffeting of the wind, short, deep shocks of sound. Looking around for the source of this unfamiliar noise, I saw a lioness lying in tawny grass not far off. She was staring intently towards the yards, full of cattle which had been enclosed for the night. She lay, ignoring me, every now and again giving over her shoulder the lioness's short gruff call to members of her pride or family. Guy joined me, and we watched her till the dusk deepened and her front was only a pale blur. Then she rose and strode into the dark. The lion himself later began to roar, almost shaking the window panes with the intensity of the sound. The lioness answered, and they kept this up well into the night.

On a stormy night some lions (presumably inexperienced) attacked our best Sahiwal milk cow, 'Neusi', which belonged to Laria. Neusi had been sleeping with her calf in a small paddock adjoining the garden, only a few yards from the house. She must have put up a gallant fight for in the morning she was still just alive, her calf untouched. Had it not been for the high wind and rain, her bellows for help would have been heard. Her calf was brought up on a bottle and grew to be one of the best herd bulls we have ever had; we named him 'Simba' (Swahili for lion). Gallant Neusi was destroyed.

Over the years a number of cattle, one horse and the children's donkey, Queenie, have been taken by lions; but that is only a tiny proportion of domestic stock in relation to their total numbers. Disease and drought have been far more significant problems in stock-raising. If, however, there were fewer wild animals, and if the stock were not 'close-*boma*-ed' at night in the traditional manner, the lions would make more use of cattle. Where there is no wild life left, or where they have lost their natural fear of man, they can be difficult and dangerous to live with, though man-eaters are uncommon in Kenya.

It is a thrilling sound, the magnificent reverberation of a lion's roaring at night. Sometimes you can hear the fierce, harsh sinews of the roars, and sometimes they are golden with distance like great plops of honey falling into jars; or so far away they are mere vibration, felt rather than heard. Though few ranchers tolerate lions, it is only on ranches and in the lands of the pastoral tribes that they and man can live in the traditional relationship of mutual respect that seems most proper.

One of the lion's prey animals is the warthog, an animal of

Heuglin's Courser
(Hemerodromus cinctus)
9ᵗʰ Aug. 1971

Found dead on track

Labiatae.

*Tinnea
aethiopica.*

*Leucas
martinicensis.*

*Leonotis
nepetifolia.*

character of which we are all particularly fond. As soon as you become used to their unusual appearance, you cannot think of them as ugly. Most of their habits and manners are interesting, amusing and attractive, though there is such a thing as a bad-tempered old boar, not averse to slashing with his tusks anything that dares stand in his burrow entrance. Most of our dogs learn to leave warthogs alone, for a sow protecting her piglets can be dangerous and an old boar is often not even comfortably approachable to dogs, though he will always run from a human that is not molesting him. Molest a warthog, however, and I would not answer for the consequences.

Once, while on an evening walk in the 'L' paddock I heard a faint keening sound which rose and fell gently, with pauses and hesitations. On creeping nearer, I saw a group of warthogs lying on their sides enjoying the evening sun. The 'keening', sometimes querulous, sometimes questioning, sometimes authoritative, was the sound of their voices in desultory conversation. I could hardly have been more surprised and entranced if they had been speaking in English, Swahili or Latin, and everything about warthogs has seemed to me to be special ever since.

Warthogs are good at digging, for which they use their tusks. The loose earth is busily pushed out of the hole with the flat of their faces, which disproves the theory that warthogs cannot turn round in their burrows. When unalarmed warthogs often go down their burrows head first, although it is quite usual for adults to back in, presumably in order to have their tusks to the fore. It is funny to see them turn smartly at the entrance in order to shoot down backwards. The burrows are not always used as boltholes in times of danger, and indeed, the more serious the danger, the more reluctant hogs seem to be to commit themselves to a burrow (lions do dig them out, and so can people). I once jumped over one that had been newly dug in the middle of a path, and in passing over saw the face of a dozing warthog at the entrance. It did not retreat farther in as one might expect, but shot straight out of the hole into the nearby river (warthogs can certainly swim), closely followed by five others which made off in different directions, while I made off in the seventh. Another time we watched a mother pig with small piglets who, when chased by dogs, led her babies to a burrow, waited till they were inside, turned round, and wedging herself like the stopper of a bottle in the entrance left only her well-armed forequarters sticking out. The dogs could do nothing and withdrew, but she did not wait in this apparently impregnable position. Instead, she led her piglets away again at a gallop while the dogs were still close by. If there had been fewer dogs she would no doubt have chased them herself, closely followed by her little ones, for we have often seen this happen. Warthogs look upon their burrows, I think, as peacetime residences: cool dark retreats from the heat of the day, or warm shelters in time of inclement weather.

Warthogs often graze on their knees, moving them along with a sliding motion while their hindlegs walk normally, their behinds comically elevated. When alarmed they carry their tails straight up, like wire aerials on small armoured cars. They can erect their manes too, when threatened, to make themselves look bigger, and also raise them and let them fall repeatedly as they move about together, probably as a means of communication.

We have seen jackals catch and kill warthog piglets, despite their mother's efforts to protect them. Nyamuluki is unusual in that all three species of jackal live here – the golden, side-striped and silver-backed – and we suspect from their appearance that they may sometimes interbreed. Of the three, we see the golden jackal least frequently. Silver-backed jackals are good hunters, taking not only piglets, but impala fawns, vervet monkeys and hares. They once killed a calf at birth, damaging the cow in the process and others killed a three-week-old calf that had got lost in the River Paddocks, but such incidents are unusual. We have not been able to work out the different ways of life of the three kinds, but have observed the side-striped and silver-backed eating the afterbirths of stock and wild animals, and their droppings often contain insect matter.

Within the last twenty years there has been one memorable explosion in the jackal population of Nyamuluki, with other minor fluctuations. When the population was at its peak, jackals could be heard calling to each other with their eerie rising yelps at all hours of the day and night, and there were as many as fourteen in the back yard every evening. The Meru people employed on Nyamuluki at the time said that, in their country, it was always considered a very bad sign when jackals called even in the daytime; and so it proved to be. The population explosion was followed by an outbreak of rabies that decimated not only the jackals, but also aardwolves, ground squirrels, hyraxes and bat-eared foxes, and posed a serious threat to people as well. We had rabid jackals and foxes in the back yard, in the garden, and twice actually in the house. Herdsmen brought in jackals they had killed after being approached by them, but luckily no one was bitten.

Sketches of Silver-backed Jackals.
(Canis mesomelas).

Jackal puppies outside den.

Family of near-adults play after rain.

NJG

Bat-eared Foxes.
(Otocyon megalotis)

Grooming cub.

Mother with cub.

Cub scratching.

Cubs.

Stretching.

A research team ear-marked some jackals with coloured plastic tags, but though quite a number were tagged, we saw only one of these animals afterwards. We suspect that their mates may have chewed the tags off almost immediately, for pairs of jackals are affectionate and concerned for each other. During the tagging operations mates hung about anxiously a few yards away, watching. Jackals are playful, too. Once they found a feather cushion which had been left on the lawn, and in the morning feathers were strewn over the nearby paddock where the jackals had had an enjoyable pillow-fight. A soft-toy horse was likewise scissored by their sharp teeth and the remains scattered far and wide, much to our smaller daughter's chagrin. And as with all intelligent animals, they show curiosity. When two of our dogs had treed a vervet monkey and were barking loudly underneath, I saw six silver-backed jackals standing around nearby. Our dogs normally chase jackals and kill them if they catch them, but they were too busy barking up the tree to notice these interested and puzzled spectators.

The bat-eared fox, though irascible, must be one of the most attractive little animals on Nyamuluki. They are, for their size, extremely brave, and often stand up in a remarkable way to dogs much bigger than themselves, sometimes quite outfacing them. However, some are killed or wounded by dogs, and they can come to each other's assistance at such times with heartrending bravery. When one of our big dogs had wounded a fox three other foxes managed, by barking, growling and nipping, to keep the dog away from the wounded one, who was accompanied by an anxious mate or litter-mate. I called the dog off with difficulty and Guy later went out with his gun to put the fox out of its pain; but it had disappeared. A few days later I found it lying dead outside a nearby den which we had already checked. Perhaps, after dying below, the other foxes had dragged its body outside.

Bat-eared foxes are sociable in spite of a certain quarrelsomeness, and we have seen as many as eleven lying together in a tight cluster outside their burrows to catch the evening sun, their twenty-two huge ears an arresting sight. Though mainly nocturnal, in the rains they often come out during the day to catch termites and to enjoy the cool, invigorating weather. At other times they come out to sunbathe. Usually they spend the heat of the day under wait-a-bit thorns or down their burrows. Sometimes when you stand near burrow entrances, you can hear their peppery little barks underground, for they know you are there and wish to see you off. Some distance from the

Bubu embarrassed by foxes.

den is a lavatorial area, and a group will go there together to leave their droppings one after another, before setting off to forage in the evening. We once opened the stomach of a fox killed by dogs, and found it to be full of the black 'sizzling' ants that not only sting most painfully, but also bite hard as well. How they manage to eat these without damage to their sensitive pink tongues, I cannot imagine.

From the garden we look along the edge of the orchard, with its vivid emerald patches of lucerne and bonner grass to the paddock beyond. One year we were lucky enough to be able to watch a family of aardwolf cubs from the lawn. They had been born in a burrow just inside this paddock fence. The aardwolf is a characteristic animal of Nyamuluki, and one that we quite often see. Like a fairy edition of the striped hyaena to look at, it is really quite different, for its teeth are insignificant and its food almost entirely insect.

The three attractive cubs in their play were like a cross between fox-cubs and kittens, yet with a kind of elegant aloofness not quite characteristic of either. They often came out of their den at tea-time, and we would watch for hours as they played and enjoyed the late sunshine. Sometimes we would creep nearer to them, hidden by bush, and once the mother came and sat down three yards from me to scratch herself, not knowing I was there. She was so close I could see the crescents of her nostrils and the grape-like bloom on her dark eyes. She seemed to get smaller the nearer she came (an effect I have noticed before with some wild creatures and birds). It is sometimes said that aardwolves are strictly nocturnal, but here that is not the case, for we have seen them out quite late in the morning and early in the afternoon.

Quite often in the paddocks one may come across a porcupine quill lying on some narrow, dusty game path, or find the porcupine's distinctive droppings beneath a desert date (*Balanites*) where they have been to eat its fruit. The nocturnal porcupine itself is less often seen, though I have met them outside their dens in the late afternoon when the sun is still shining. On an afternoon walk in the 'L' paddock I saw two baby porcupines playing outside a hole that was once occupied by aardwolves. They must have heard me, for they bundled down the hole, their already stiffened quills abristle. They were most attractive miniatures of the adults.

A particularly astute, quick-witted, and gallant small animal found not only in the paddocks, but all over Nyamuluki, is the African hare. It is subject to population fluctuations like those of the jackal, though the connection, if any, between these

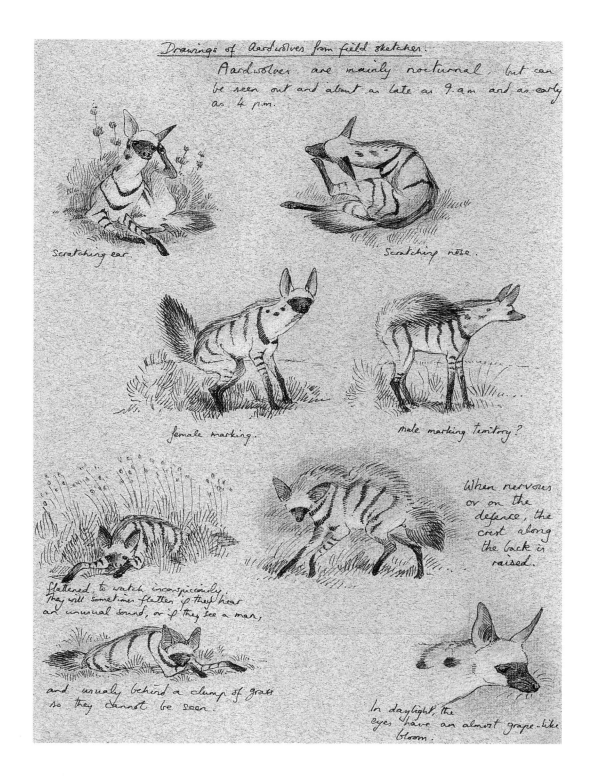

Drawings of Aardwolves from field sketches.

Aardwolves are mainly nocturnal, but can be seen out and about as late as 9 am and as early as 4 p.m.

Scratching ear.

Scratching nose.

female marking.

male marking territory?

When nervous or on the defence, the crest along the back is raised.

flattened, to watch inconspicuously, they will sometimes flatten if they hear an unusual sound, or if they see a man,

and usually behind a clump of grass so they cannot be seen.

In daylight, the eyes have an almost grape-like bloom.

from sketches of African hares
done from life.

alert.

zig-zagging.

alert.

observing.

nervous.

floating bound.

population changes in the two animals is not obvious to us. The year we had the 'explosion' of jackals there was a hare which had its form near the dip, and it was there every day in spite of the great numbers of its primary predators. We have seen pairs of jackals coursing hares on a number of occasions, sometimes successfully. Our dogs hunt hares too, but nearly always the hares get away through a combination of speed and strategy. The deaths by dog that we witness are due to bad luck: for instance a dog coming unexpectedly from the opposite direction or a hare going to ground in an accessible spot because of inexperience or unfitness. Jackals are faster than most dogs, and so more dangerous to hares.

An old pointer bitch of ours, Tess, although slower than her pack mates, was still able to point out game. The other dogs, seeing her standing stock-still in characteristic pose, like a lanky, painted wooden toy with a stick on a hinge for a tail, would rush over to her to put up whatever it may have been and give chase. If it was only birds they were clearly disgusted, but if it was a hare, they went off at top speed, Tess following behind as fast as she was able. The hare would stay just in front, every now and again doing a stupendous, floating bound with its tail aloft like a black and white banner. It seemed to pace the dogs, going only so fast as was necessary to stay in front. Suddenly, it would double back and, putting on a great spurt, was already halfway to a known refuge before the dogs had managed to brake and turn around. This doubling back is always timed and directed to avoid flanking dogs, and to do it the hare must look behind it out of the corners of its big eyes to ascertain the position of each pack member. Hares often sit tight in the open while dogs go past, and then sneak off in another direction. Once, a hare dodged around some clumps of grass with surprising sang-froid in front of a dog's nose, round and round, in and out, obviously hoping the dog would 'mislay' it. In the end though, it had to break cover and run.

Another tactic we have witnessed more than once is used when two dogs are running on either side of the hare, only a little way behind it. Suddenly the hare stops dead in front of a bush or grass clump and doubles back at lightning speed. The two dogs, going flat out, shoot past the bush on either side, and it is some seconds before they realise that the hare is no longer in front of them. Sometimes a hare will run repeatedly through a bunch of cattle, which scatter when the dogs reach them and put them off their stride, so allowing the hare to escape.

African hare.

It must not be thought that we encourage our dogs to course hares, but it is absolutely no use trying to call them off for they are too excited to hear – or if they do hear they may imagine we are yelping encouragement. When they return they are far too cheerful and unsuccessful to be punished.

We have also seen tawny eagles hunting hares. Once there was a long chase as the quarry galloped up the hill on the track from Cheetah Corner to Toru, the eagle flying along just behind it a few feet from the ground. They disappeared over the crest of the hill, and by the time we arrived the eagle was sitting on the body of the unfortunate animal and had already begun its meal. Eagles must be one of the greatest dangers to the hare in daytime, but other predators include large puff-adders who can swallow them whole, and eagle-owls, servals and caracals. Perhaps it is not surprising that the hare is quick-witted, for only the quick-witted survive.

Many Africans believe that the hare consumes dung of other animals, and for this reason will not themselves eat its meat. We have not yet seen this, and I sometimes wonder if the belief stems from the fact that hares and rabbits excrete special soft dottles which they reingest in order that the food they contain can be properly digested. Only after this second passage, are the now hard, dry dottles abandoned.

In the paddocks in front of the house we see herds of eland, impala, zebra and giraffe, and can even watch them from the house itself. Female giraffes often give birth in these paddocks, perhaps feeling that the proximity of people will deter predators. But this habit proves to be a mistake, for once the calves are weaned they will not leave the paddock because of the fence around it, over which their mothers step with ease. Even young giraffes tall enough to step over it, sometimes do not. When the dry weather comes and the leaves of the thorn trees in the paddocks nearly disappear, the youngsters begin to starve. We have tried driving them out, but as soon as they reach the place where the fence had stood they often stop and turn at bay, or gallop back the way they have come. This behaviour always puzzles us and we have had some deaths because of it. Perhaps ungulates find it hard to focus on wire, and know it is there only when they come into contact with it, and sometimes assume it is there when it is not. Recently we saw a herd of eland leap over a non-existent 'wire' when they came to a line of old fence posts which had not been wired for over twenty years.

Sadly, too, some giraffes are snared by poachers hunting for meat and, in the past, for their tail tufts (hair from the tails was

Impressions of Impalas
from sketches

Civet.
Viverra civetta
(*Civetictis civetta*)

used for bracelets and charms). The poachers erect huge cable-like nooses of twisted wire between trees overhanging paths used by giraffes. Guy has had to shoot those giraffes that have somehow managed to break loose, but still have these devilish wires biting deep into their necks.

Occasionally while out walking you may hear a sound like that of an animal dragging in its last breaths through an obstructed throat – a kind of small, groaning roar. When I first heard this I thought something was caught in a snare. The sound seemed to be coming from the ground, and the nearer I got, the louder it became till suddenly it was right at my feet. I looked down in astonishment, for it was a pair of mating tortoises. Perhaps the male makes this noise to impress the female, for if mating were such an effort, tortoises would surely have been extinct long ago? Tortoises, rather against expectations, are quite lively reptiles. We have a pair living near the house who mate nearly every day, and sometimes twice a day (perhaps even more often when we are not looking) during the rainy season. The male, which is half the size of the female, follows her around, every now and again thumping the back of her shell with the front of his own, as if to chivy her along faster. Sometimes the female steps over an obstacle that defeats the smaller male. By the time he has found his way around it, the female may be out of sight, and it is amusing to watch him hurrying about with his head in the air, or sniffing the ground, in his efforts to find her again. We have seen this female swallowing small pieces of bone, perhaps to help in forming shells for the eggs she was soon to lay.

Though tortoises are frisky in the new green grass of the rains, in the dry weather they become slow and torpid, sometimes even aestivating. The female tortoise has a convex underside, and the male a concave one, so that his shell will fit better the curve of the female's back during mating. But I think it is a mistake to look under a tortoise during the dry weather in order to see what sex it is, for they often empty their bladders in fear or defence. This water in the bladder might be a useful source of moisture in the body of the tortoise and it may die if it loses it.

Night comes fast on Nyamuluki, for it is an equatorial night. As the sky takes on the soft french blue of dusk and the full moon, like a huge golden doubloon, floats free of the horizon – almost leaps free, for you can see it move – the noises of the night begin to be heard. Perhaps there is a hyaena's distant whoop like a question repeated five times in gradual diminuendo until lost in a growl, or the harsh squalling of a pair of

courting white-tailed mongooses. The night-time cicadas and crickets strike up their buzz and trill, while Heuglin's coursers and spotted stone curlews chuckle and bubble. Perhaps there are the hoofbeats, muffled in sand, of a startled giraffe as it sways out of the trees at a rocking canter, its form only dimly seen in the growing dark. Nightjars call 'chucker-chucker' from the ground, or sweep in mothy circuits against the sky, while the day's last tantrum, from a sleepy baboon child, may be heard from the river.

I am walking home through the paddocks, to lamplight glowing warm and dusky apricot, the same colour as the after-glow of the sunset against which, a few minutes earlier, the house and its trees had been silhouetted. As I go into the house, the night people are leaving their dens and roosts – elusive civet, lithe genet, white-tailed mongoose, bat, moth and owl. How alien and blinding the harsh white light of day must seem to creatures used to gentle, friendly darkness and the soft light of the moon and stars. How sweet the white flowers that open at night must smell to them. How much we miss by sleeping all night!

White-tailed Mongoose (*Ichneumia albicauda.*)

Dusky Nightjar. (male)
(*Caprimulgus pectoralis.*)
Life size.

This side not coloured in.

Killed by car. Rumuruti Road
7th Feb. 1987.

Anacardiaceae.

Rhus quartiniana.

May '92

July 92

· 4 ·
The river and gullies

The River Uaso Nyiro (meaning 'dark water' in Maasai) is the lifeline of Nyamuluki. When the gullies, and later the dams, have dried, it is the only source of water for our stock and for the wild animals, very few of which can do entirely without drinking. In the dry weather the river sometimes dwindles to a fifth or less of its normal capacity, and flows sluggishly between its steep banks. It no longer sparkles and sings in the rocky places, and the river vegetation drops its wrinkled yellow leaves to float slowly on the surface amongst dapples of scum. Hippos are furtive in the deeper pools, and the bushbuck crackles the dry undergrowth as he picks his way through his home thickets. At midday the air sizzles with heat, and birds pant in the thin shade.

Later, as the softness of the evening develops and chalk-blue shadows lengthen over the parched ground, the heat seeps away, and buffalo leave the mukinyea thickets on the slopes and forge their way to secret drinking places at the river. In the morning there are glossy blue-black pats and large cloven tracks to tell of their coming, and you can see where they have dragged their feet through the grasses in their ponderous progress.

But a buffalo can move with wicked quickness when it wants to, and it is the buffalo that we fear most to meet when walking through thick bush. There is no doubt that a female buffalo with a new calf, if come upon suddenly, will charge before asking questions, and one of the Nyamuluki herdsmen was gored in the groin by such a cow. Though a wounded buffalo bull is reputed to be amongst the most intelligent and dangerous non-human adversaries a man can have, ordinarily they are rather peace-loving animals, and will usually move off

Olive baboon. Papio anubis.

if they know you are there. However, they become bolder as dusk draws on, and more likely to investigate a disturbance. One of our *boma* dogs, Naibor ('white' in Maasai) saved the life of his shepherd when a lame buffalo bull charged out at him without warning. Naibor jumped at it, barking, holding it at bay while the shepherd escaped. Guy later shot this bull. Another herdsman was pinned to the ground by his thigh by a bull that had been hiding in an isolated bush, and was probably only saved by a companion who fired his shot-gun into the air, thus frightening off the buffalo. People on neighbouring properties have been killed by wounded buffaloes, and the great, solid creatures are best given a wide berth and left in peace.

All through the dry weather, guinea-fowls live in flocks, sometimes of over a hundred strong. Shallow basins pit the ground where they have scratched their dust-baths or dug up the bulbs of onion-grass, and their beautiful white-spotted feathers lie on the ground like messages in an unknown code. Every evening they hurry towards the river 'chinking' and 'tsinking' gently to each other. Finally they rise up together with a clangour of metallic cries and glide on curved wings to the tops of the riverside yellow-thorns, there to balance and scold until settled for the night.

Olive baboons sleep in the same trees, although often they do not bother to ascend till well after dusk, for they do not particularly fear the leopard (though they will set up a staccato of double barks if one passes beneath their tree in the night). A leopard is no match for a group of baboons, and knows it, for the large males of the troop are extremely brave and ready to give their lives for their families. One of our dogs was killed, and others have been seriously wounded, by baboons, and the dogs have killed them, but in every case the dogs were the first aggressors.

Many people think of baboons as unattractive creatures with habits that make them appear, somehow, caricatures of human beings. I, too, felt something of this until Laria, with her love of and interest in the baboons forced me to observe them properly. Then I saw how the mature males create an atmosphere of dignity, assurance, peaceful power and tolerance. I saw too how well-ordered and quiet is the baboons' social organisation; how peacefully they coexist within their close-knit society. There is, of course, the odd serious confrontation, childish tantrum, juvenile quarrel or social disruption, but the strongest feeling they impart to me is one of great tranquillity.

In times of plenty, baboons do not have to forage all day for

Baboon children in rain.

Sketches from life.

Alarm call is a short gruff bark.

Alert female.

Move secretively, mostly in morning and evening.

White marking varies a lot with individuals. Some have very little, others are heavily marked.

Wags tail nervously at intervals as it walks.

Males become progressively darker with age.

Bushbuck,
(Tragelaphus scriptus)

Turns up white underside of tail when in flight.

food, and much of their time is spent enjoying family life and the sunshine, grooming each other, playing and snoozing. In the mornings they do not hurry down from their roost trees, but wait for the sun to warm them through and through, before making a leisurely descent.

Roosting vultures, also, wait for the ground to warm before flapping heavily from their perches to find a rising thermal of air to soar on. Though other birds can glide, vultures are masters of the art. Their gliding is without ostentation, apparently utterly effortless and of a casual, unhurried grace that takes one's breath away with admiration and envy. Perhaps the gentle, other-worldly lustre of a vulture's eyes comes from the sea-ways of space and its utter freedom to roam them. But, in spite of magnificence in flight, vultures are terribly smelly birds, though they like to be clean. We have watched them bathing with touching earnestness and care, and it was obvious that they enjoyed the water.

Morning sunlight may reveal a leopard's neat pug marks strung along a river path. There have always been plenty of them on Nyamuluki except during those years of maximum

3. Lappet-faced

1. Ruppell's Griffon

2. White-backed

4. Egyptian

Vultures on a lion kill. Giraffe Ridge with Nyamuluki Hill in the background.

demand for leopard-skin coats, when poachers were at work throughout the country. Since then leopards have re-established a healthy population and their rasping 'saw' is often heard at night from the direction of the river. From a distance this call sounds rather as if someone is sawing wet wood inside a grand piano, but nearby it is a thrilling crescendo of short throaty roars, capable of lifting the hairs on the back of one's neck.

Leopards also frequent the seasonal water courses and wooded gullies that cross the rolling plains, and sometimes at night they will leave these to inspect a *boma* of sheep and goats. Occasionally they jump in and bodily remove one of its occupants, but are not always successful if the shepherd's dog gives warning. We had a *boma* dog called Charlie who attacked one such marauding leopard and saw it off at the cost of some deep gashes in his own hide. While these were sewn up, without benefit of anaesthetic or tranquilisers, he uttered not a single squeak of complaint. Luckily he recovered quickly without infection.

Leopards will take calves, and have done so from the cattle-yards just below the house in spite of dogs, fires and sleeping herdsmen nearby. The skull I have drawn was of the last leopard to be shot on Nyamuluki, over twenty years ago. It was a very large male who had become a regular calf-killer, taking big, eight-month-old weaners, and finally even a lame two-

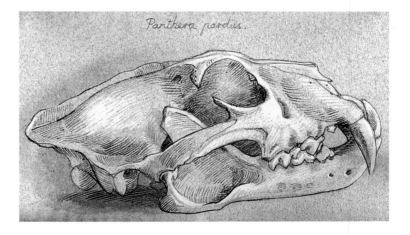

Panthera pardus.

year-old steer. Since then, no leopard has been shot, the few that were serious nuisances having been moved to National Parks and released. The loss of a few sheep and goats to leopards each year seems to us an acceptable price to pay for a land still healthy and diverse enough to support its own predators.

Recently we set the box trap for a calf-killer in the River Paddock below the yards, and in four successive nights we caught three different leopards. We guessed that the first two were a mother and her fully-grown son (these were released together), and the third was an adult female who was let out there and then, as she was deemed too small to be guilty of calf-killing. Translocation is not altogether satisfactory, as we do not know what happens to a leopard thus removed from all that is familiar, and released into the established territories of strange leopards. Many may try to come home, and some young leopards may depend on their mothers to provide food long after they are apparently capable of fending for themselves. But the leopard is an adaptable creature, and I expect that many survive.

Usually leopards keep to their secretive ways and hunt their favourite bushbuck prey, the remains of which we sometimes see hanging in trees. We have also found a zebra foal hung up, and two or three white-tailed mongoose skulls perforated by leopard's teeth, and often we come upon their twisted droppings full of bushbuck and impala hair, with fragments of bone.

Many years ago meat would be fixed in a leaning tree at the lower end of Leopard Ridge and we would spend the night there in an old wagon, watching for leopards. A hurricane lantern was suspended in the tree near the meat, to light the leopard as it came to feed. When it left, as silently as a wraith of mist, one could not help wondering if it was coming to look in at the open end of the wagon. We stopped this practice at the time of poaching, for it made things only too easy for the poachers.

Sometimes in the early morning during the green weather, the river course is hidden by a soft, white ground-mist through which only the very tops of the yellow-thorns appear, mysterious above it. The grass, drenched with heavy dew drops is pale as frosted jade, and patterned with the tracks of animals in a richer, darker green. Spiders' webs in the grass are like sheets of mother-of-pearl, made almost solid by the condensed breath of humidity, and refracting the light into the colours of milky opal when the sun catches them. In years of good rain the vegetation near the river grows fast and thick until sometimes the place seems quite unfamiliar, with paths grown over, bushes unrecognisable and the grass matted and knee high. When the river is in spate, it does not roar and thunder like a Scottish burn, but rolls along with a faint hissing, its milky terracotta surface roiling and braiding with the powerful current. In rocky places the water shouts, but with a rushing sound rather than a roar, for the rocks are all smothered beneath a great weight of water.

One day when the gullies were running with freshets of rainwater, we saw the migration of clawed toads. Murray and some of his friends, with a dog called Worra, had hurried off to the First Gully to play in the water. After a while he came galloping back, calling excitedly, 'Look what Worra has killed!' and pulled something from the back pocket of his shorts by an incredibly long, yellow hind leg. It was a clawed toad a strangely flattened creature with muscular hind legs and embryonic-looking front ones. As we stared it began to twitch and revive, so, putting it in a little water in the bottom of a bucket, we took it back to the gully. There, the other small boys were shouting with excitement, for in the water thousands of these toads were swimming upstream and coming out on stones and onto the banks to rest. The gully was packed with them, and there was a strong fishy smell hanging over it. Once we were used to their odd and initially repulsive appearance, we found them not unpleasant creatures. They varied in colour from dark greenish-black to almost pure white, some being pale khaki, some brown or a pale reddish colour, while others were mottled or spotted. However every one was bright yellow underneath. Though they had black claws on their inner toes, they did not scratch when picked up, and felt almost boneless in one's hand. Were they migrating from the river? To where? And why? Had they just come from their aestivation mud beds? There was something distinctly Permian about them. I feel sure that this migration must happen often though we have seen it only once.

When rain has soaked the land and water is lying in the dams and gullies, frogs set up a roar of croaking at night which can be heard for miles around, carried on the breeze in swelling gusts of sound. Tree-frogs pipe musically like small bells. Spawn is laid and tadpoles hatch out and develop quickly, for no water is permanent here, except in the river. But along the river, frogs are to be seen all year round, throwing themselves like small javelins into the water from the grassy banks with every step you take.

Brown freshwater crabs are also found in the river, and the

Fresh water crab.

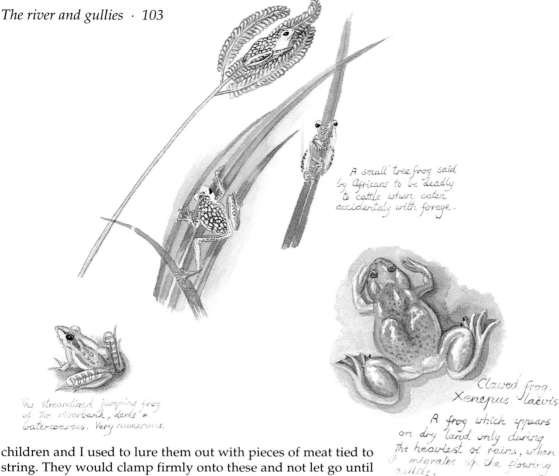

A small tree frog said by Africans to be deadly to cattle when eaten accidentaly with forage.

Clawed frog.
Xenopus laevis.

A frog which appears on dry land only during the heaviest of rains, when it migrates up the flowing gullies.

The streamlined jumping frog of the riverbank, dams & watercourses. Very numerous.

children and I used to lure them out with pieces of meat tied to string. They would clamp firmly onto these and not let go until drawn onto the bank, when they would scuttle back into the water. In recent years the Louisiana crayfish, brought into the country and released, has somehow found its way to the river and become naturalised. Both these creatures are relished by, and form the staple diet of, the large Cape clawless otter which lives in the river and leaves its shell-filled spraints on strategic rocks along its course. We find the otter's childlike tracks, of mobile-fingered hands and long web-toed feet, in the mud, but they are extremely elusive creatures.

Late one afternoon Guy saw what he described as the 'flat, catty little face' of an otter as it swam down a quiet stretch of the river, and visitors to our camp have occasionally seen them. I am still waiting for my first view in the wild of what I know to be an attractive and intelligent personage, for I have met tame clawless otters elsewhere.

There are no crocodiles in the river where it flows past Nyamuluki, though there are some not far downstream, at a lower altitude. Perhaps the water is too cold for them here,

Clawless Otter. (*Aonyx capensis.*)

coming as it does from the Aberdare Mountains and being joined by a smaller river originating in the snows of Mount Kenya. However, monitor lizards which sometimes reach a length of six feet or even more, live along the bank. Usually they see you before you see them, and with a heavy splash dive into the water to swim soundlessly downstream. We often see their long-toed tracks in the mud, and the grooves made by their tails dragging behind.

Here is an extract from my diary:

> *December 3, 1985.* We went down to the weir. There was a huge monitor lizard on the squiggly rocks on the far side of the pool. He hurried clumsily along, looking like a small crocodile, and disappeared in the under-growth upstream. He must have been at least six feet long, and had a wavy wrinkle, or fold of skin, along his side. One could hear (or did I only fancy one could hear?) the dry plops of his feet above the roar of water coming through the weir!

There always used to be tree hyraxes along the river, and at night we would hear them calling to each other with extraordinary ratchet-like grunts which were followed by a series of diminishing screams and screeches. Sometimes we caught, glimpses of their dark, furry figures scampering up perpen-

The old weir.

Rock Hyrax (Procavia capensis) on Long Rocks.

dicular branches, or galloping along horizontal ones, but they came out mostly at night.

At the Ravine, and on the Long Rocks not far from the river, there were always rock hyraxes. It was fun to watch these intelligent and sociable animals playing, or lying out in the sun like little bears. But in 1981, the year of the worst drought and of the outbreak of rabies, both the rock and tree hyraxes disappeared. We do not know if they contracted rabies or some other disease, or died of starvation caused by the drought. It is possible that they may have migrated, for we found no dead hyraxes, and there were two pathetic stragglers, one on the office roof in the farmyard, and the other in the orchard – both totally unsuitable places for hyraxes and far from their normal haunts. Rock hyraxes have only just begun to return along the river from rocks and kopjes downstream, and any night now we expect to hear again a tree hyrax scream, for many still live

Tiliaceae.

Grewia similis.

Fruits edible, but
each with, large, single.
"stone".

June '92

Aug '92.

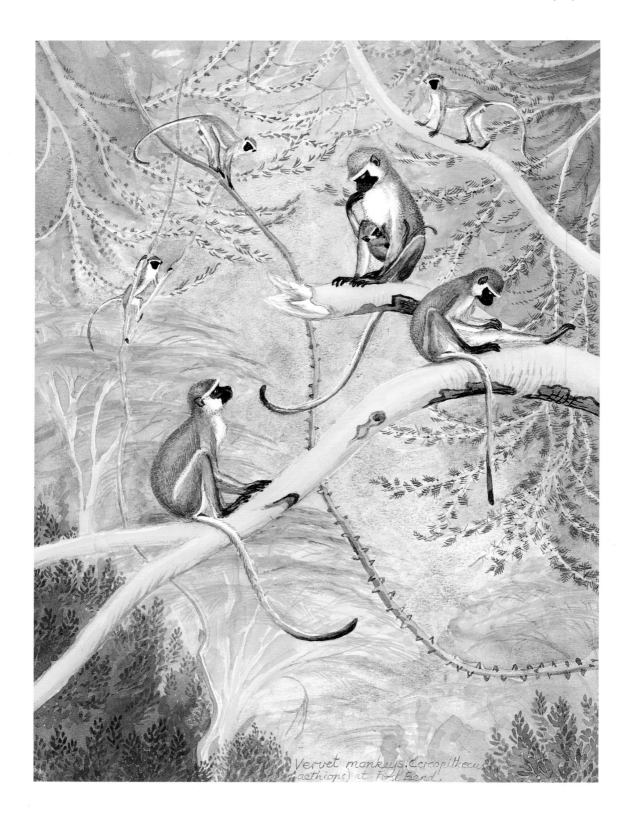

Vervet monkeys (Cercopithecus aethiops) at First Bend.

in the forests upstream. They have taken, though, a surprisingly long time to come back.

As the gullies that traverse Nyamuluki finally approach the river, they become more winding, more steeply banked, and over arched by the saffron limbs of tall yellow-thorn trees. The beds of these gullies, when not filled with running water, are of pale sand, and quite level. There is something very peaceful, secret and restful about these winding, shaded corridors so smoothly floored, and sunk below the level of the surrounding land. Suspended above them are the small green onions of the vitelline masked weavers' nests, and the elongated twiggy baskets of the red-headed weavers. Along their beds are footprints left by wandering hippos, or of buffalo which have crossed from one side to the other in the night, the handprints of baboons and bushbuck's narrow slots. Sometimes there are the momentous talismen of lion pugmarks, and one is never quite sure what may be around the next mysterious bend. For this reason we seldom walk along these sand luggahs (seasonal watercourses). Their quietness is only emphasised by the electronic callnote of grey-backed camaroptera moving in overhanging thickets, or the half-toned counting of the sulphur-breasted bush shrike. Sometimes you may see a flock of black and white crested helmet-shrikes fly through the overhead tree canopy and far above them a gliding bateleur eagle passing quickly over, like a boomerang.

At the river, itself, a pair of hammerkops might bob to each other on the roof of their huge tree cabin of sticks, while vervet monkeys feed on acacia blossom. Below, a Peter's finfoot, swimming low in the water like a cormorant, its tail spread fan-wise on the surface, may be moving in and out among the clumps of water plants below the bank, propelled by its huge orange feet. Perhaps a pair of black river ducks, decorated with crescent moons of white, float, lazily preening their wings and breasts. If you disturb them, the finfoot, rowing with his wings in a flurry of water, will disappear; the river ducks will fly fast and low around the next bend; the vervets will scold with a sound reminiscent of the whirring of football supporters' rattles, and the hammerkops will rise like a pair of brown pterodactyls to flit silently away.

Black-headed heron   Ardea melanocephalis

· 5 ·

The dams and the open bush

The open bush stretches from beyond the house and pad-docks to the north, and does not stop in that direction till eventually it merges with the Sahara. If you sit quietly on the hill of Nyamuluki ('watchtower' in the language of the Meru tribe), which sometimes seems to be the heart of the ranch, you may feel the breeze coming and going gently. It seems like the breath of Nyamuluki itself. From the hill the horizons form a circle around you, except where Mount Kenya rises to its white, glacier-tipped cone away to the south-east. One of the lovely things about the bushland of Nyamuluki are the long, subtle swells of its horizons: how the bow-like line of one contrasts with the curve of another, yet merges with it at the same time. The tensions of these lines make for a horizon that is never monotonous, and each high, open ridgetop has its own beauty and character. Nestled at the feet of these curving downs are the four dams which attract a great deal of wildlife while they contain water.

In the dams live turtles which I imagine must have got there first by travelling up the gullies from the river. In the dry weather they must bury themselves in the mud of the bottom, alongside aestivating frogs and lung-fish. We once saw a dab-chick struggling with its head under water, but by the time we reached it a turtle had killed it. They must be a lurking menace to many birds, for the dams always have their complement of ducks, geese and waders, both migratory and local, all of which seem happily unaware of the carnivorous turtle.

Each dam provides a perfect stage for watching these birds. At the water's edge snipe sedately probe the mud, pushing their long beaks in nearly up to the their eyes. Black-winged stilts, high-stepping their stick-like coral legs in the shallows,

lean forward to swing their beaks hesitantly just below the surface. Sturdy white spoonbills, striding along in deeper water, scythe purposefully from side to side, regular as machinery. Marsh sandpipers use the same movement speeded up while they hurry along the edge, as if they will be flying off to catch a train at any moment. Now and again dabchicks bob up like coloured ping-pong balls from forays below the surface, water rolling from their oily and incredibly thick feather coats in round, silver droplets. From the reeds and sedges under the dam wall the breathy trumpet-and-boom of surreptitious black crakes can be heard, while from above may fall the wild, lonely cry of a solitary greenshank – the most lovely of sounds. Sometimes pelicans fish in the dams, looking rather like flotillas of bath toys as they plunge their yellow fishing bags below

Some Plovers & Waders + Stilt.

Senegal plovers. (Vanellus lugubris)
local migrants, appear with the rain.

Crowned plovers. (Vanellus coronatus)
Resident all year.

detail of
head.

Three-banded plovers.
(Charadrius tricolaris)
Resident.

Caspian plovers. ♂ ♀ (Charadrius asiaticus)
Migratory. (Winter visitor from palearctic)
Seen in March on way North.

Blacksmith plovers. (Vanellus armatus)
Resident with local movements. A few
pairs present only when dams contain water.

Common sandpiper.
(Actitis hypoleucos)
Palearctic migrant. Present
all non-breeding season.

Black-winged stilt (Himantopus himantopus)
Migrant and resident.
Visit dams when they contain water.

Greenshank (Tringa nebularia)
Palearctic migrant. Visits dams
in passing.

the surface in unison. On the shore short-legged common sandpipers potter and stints shoot along in smooth fits and starts as if on castors. There used often to be migrants such as pintail and shoveller duck, and every year hundreds of European white storks came spiralling in great vortices from the sky, turning like chaff caught in slow whirlpools, but now we seldom see more than a dozen together. For some years two rare black storks visited us, but lately only one, alone and bedraggled.

It was near Murera, the biggest of the dams, that 'Gyppy', the Egyptian goose, hatched out of his egg in June 1979. Two days later, he was kidnapped. A herdsman had seen him with his family and, with mistaken kindness, had captured the gosling and brought him proudly home for our children. It was, we thought, too late to return him to the dam, for night was coming on. Luckily, one of our Muscovy ducks had ducklings about the same size as Gyppy (though older), so we put the gosling under her and she seemed to accept him at once as her own.

In spite of this, the next day he ran endlessly up and down on his proportionately very long legs, leaning forward at an angle and rolling from side to side like an exhausted long-distance runner, squeaking for his mother. The ducklings observed him with astonishment, but seemed to accept him as a queer addition to the family. At this stage Gyppy's back was covered in soft, dark grey down with two white spots on either side, while his underside was cream. As he was still very young it was clear that he would need brooding, but the ducklings had got beyond that stage and as the mother duck did not offer to do the job, I did. At regular intervals through the day, and for many days thereafter, I would catch him and hold him under my shirt, where he would at once collapse into an exhausted sleep for ten to fifteen minutes, to awake refreshed.

That first day we did not see him eat, but on the second he took some green leaves from weeds we provided, and by the third day he was feeding on regular duck food with the others. From then on he only looked forward.

Gyppy was, from an early age, bossy with other poultry. He would walk boldly up to them with his head down and his beak open, showing the pink inside. If that did not intimidate them, he would let out a sudden high-pitched squeak, as if he had been squeezed sharply. This always took effect, and it was funny to see the others jump into the air with the shock of the sound, before retreating from so small and immature a bird. Gyppy always looked rather surprised himself. He was diffi-

Gyppy.

dent, however, with his 'mother' and three 'brothers' at meal times, though he led the family in terms of exploration, ingenuity and enterprise.

Three months later Gyppy's beautiful feathers were coming in fast and he increased in elegance every day. His long legs began to take on a rosy blush. By now he and his family had freedom to come and go where and when they chose, as does every bird in the poultry flock once it has passed the vulnerable stage of chickhood, and Gyppy spent his time marching delicately about the runs and yard. After a bath he would do a wild, spooky dance, and it was at this time, when his wings (now resplendent with a shot-silk speculum of mauve and green) were outspread, that he discovered he could fly. Being so light, he would take off almost involuntarily when a headwind blew. One day Laria saw him pass over the house, and we all ran out in time to see him make a perilous landing in the back yard.

His test flights were amusing to watch. All the while hissing

Sketch of Black dam with spoonbills and Egyptian geese. Late afternoon. April 89.

Looking South-West from High Ridge towards Aberdare Mountains. Dry weather.

and honking with excitement, and hurtling through the air at rather low altitude, he would come in for landings that we felt were much too fast. He had a comical expression of anxiety on his face just before touchdown, and from the front one could see him tipping steeply first to one side then the other, like an unsteady pupil-flown aircraft doing 'bumps and circuits'. He always seemed terribly pleased with himself after these thrilling excursions, and strutted about honking. The hens, ducks and geese appeared to take no notice whatsoever of his flights, but he did influence them. The Muscovy ducks took to flying more than they had done before or ever did again when he had left.

At night Gyppy slept with his three brothers, now large drakes. If accidentally shut up by himself he would go into a frenzy, beating himself against the wire, but as soon as he was joined by even one of his adoptive siblings, he would calm down. Later, the family was moved to the large duck-house with the rest of the flock, and this seemed to be an acceptable arrangement.

In the green weather Gyppy perfected his flying, but as soon as the dry weather set in he stayed in the yard with the others. Then one afternoon in April 1980, just after the next rains had begun, we heard Egyptian geese honking near the hen runs. We went out to see two wild geese looking in at Gyppy, who appeared to be taking little notice except that he was showing the white of his shoulders: always a sign of excitement. The wild ones seemed to be doing some kind of display for his benefit, standing up tall, breast to breast, showing their white shoulders and puffing out their necks and hissing. Then they marched up and down one behind the other, the smaller of the two hissing continuously. Later they chased the ducks, and Gyppy himself. He took tactful evasive action, and seemed not unduly ruffled. These meetings and social interactions with his own kind continued through the rest of the year, but I do not think he took them very seriously. He still thought he was a duck.

In November of that year, Gyppy had an identity crisis. He attempted to mate with a Muscovy duck. When she refused to cooperate he flew into a rage and attacked her savagely, pulling out a lot of her wing feathers and causing her to bleed badly from the stubs. He became morose and withdrawn. By now he was fully grown, heavier, with glossy plumage, coral legs, and a chestnut ring round the base of his neck. He did not try to mate with a duck again, and by April 1981, when the grass was once more green, he was ready to go wild. He absented himself for longer periods, and began to stay away at night, though most mornings he would fly over the house. There were many wild Egyptian geese around, and from May onwards, he stayed away permanently. We wished we had put a ring on his leg, for it was impossible after that to be sure which of the wild geese he was. We hoped he survived and raised families of his own. Geese are long-lived birds, and for all we know, he may still be alive.

The Black Dam, named for the colour of the earth around it, lies in a wide, bowl-like hollow of grassland dotted with whistling thorns. To the north-east, beyond the dam wall, one can see over woods of mukinyea to the Three Hills and the Loldaiga Hills, but there are no trees around the dam itself, and the blue sky, mirrored on its surface, is unbroken by other reflections. Sometimes it looks like a hole in the land going straight through to more sky on the other side, and reflections

of birds flying over its surface are like other birds swooping up
to meet them from that sky below. When rainstorms bruise the
horizon, alpine and mottled swifts cut through the air with a
sound like sheets being ripped, and their crescent forms swoop
down to the dam and cause plumes of white water to appear
and disappear as they accelerate again into the sky. They come
and go so fast that I can never make out if they are taking a
drink, scooping a floating insect, or having a split-second bath
in passing. Sometimes they hawk over the high plains catching
winged termites, and with them we have seen the little hobby
falcon hardly larger than they are. Flocks of migrating kestrels
and white-eyed kestrels, and occasionally flocks of sooty fal-
cons also make use of the flying termites over the plains of
Nyamuluki. Termites must be of enormous importance to
many birds and mammals, for they appear at the beginning of
the rains after a long period of dearth, and just before migration. The birds can fatten quickly on the termites' nourishing
protein before starting their journeys north.

Shortly before the rains come termites bring up damp earth

Ant hill.   . Sept '91.   A typical termite hill. After the August rain.

Compositae.

Kleinia kleinioides.

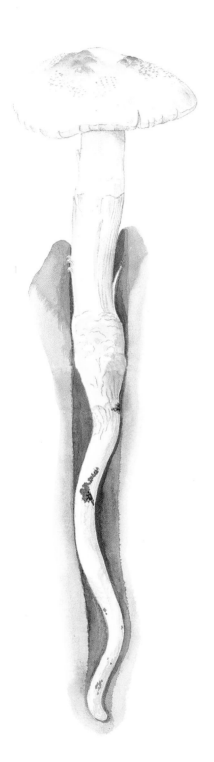

from deep down in the ground to add to the outside of their hills, which during the dry season have become smooth and worn. This is one of the surest signs that rain is expected. The new building is very easy to see, as it has a rougher texture and darker colour than the old surfaces. During the rains they continue to build, and many new funnels appear in the ground and gradually coalesce. After heavy rain, winged termites, male and female, come out in their thousands from special crescent-shaped doorways made for them by the workers in the ground around these hills. They spout into the cool air in silver fountains, like an exodus of fairies from their magic knowes, and we have seen all manner of birds feeding on them, from warblers to eagles. White-tailed mongooses and bat-eared foxes come out in the daylight to enjoy them, and toads gorge themselves, using their hands to help stuff the insects into their mouths.

The termites drift up into the sky and away, later to come down in some new place. There, the females fervently fan their four wings until the males find them, and once a male has taken up position behind the female of his choice, they both at once break off their wings at special fracture lines and start to walk in close tandem, so they will not become separated. They walk until they find a soft place in the damp earth in which to dig a chamber, mate, and raise their first brood together. It is fascinating to walk about after a heavy rain and see the termites fanning their wings on the ground, on grass stems and twigs, and to see the hundreds of little pairs dancing the conga as they go off to found new homes. There is the very faintest rustling all around you as others fly through the air, and later the discarded, silvery wings are sometimes blown into drifts along the edges of paths and tracks, or form a lacy mosaic on the surface of puddles.

Termites are important, too, in aerating and maintaining soil fertility, for they chew up dead wood and take it down into the earth to form gardens where they grow the fungus that isa their sole food. So every piece of dead wood collected for firewood is so much less nutrient returned to the earth. Often if you bump into a dead branch or tree in the bush, there is a loud ticking noise. It is made by the soldier termites knocking their heads against the nearest hard surface as a warning to the others.

Dung beetles of many kinds are seen during the rains. Often in pairs, they make balls of animal dung which they roll over the ground looking for a suitable place in which to bury the ball. Often one beetle will climb on top of the ball of dung and

from sketches of a White-tailed
mongoose enjoying termites

Nov. 89.

Growing at edges of termite hills.
Cap opening flatter later.

April 89.

dry and disappear
very quickly in sunshine.

Mushroom.

In short grass or on bare
ground.

Open grassy areas.   Nov. '88.

Fungae.

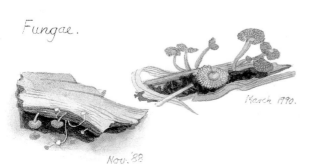

March 1990.

Nov. '88.

Grow from beneath bark
on dead wood.

Underside.

NJC

Grows on
dung.
Nov. 88.
V. slight
aniseed smell.

May 1st 89.
In hollow tree stump.

May '89.
growing in shade
on contents of disturbed
termite mound, over an
area of some square yards.
Strong mealy smell.

April '89.

on log.

Underside.

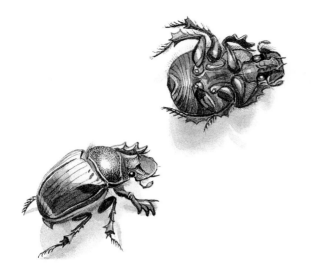

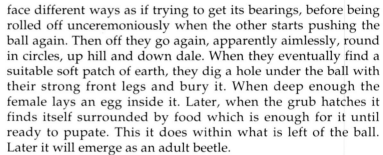

face different ways as if trying to get its bearings, before being rolled off unceremoniously when the other starts pushing the ball again. Then off they go again, apparently aimlessly, round in circles, up hill and down dale. When they eventually find a suitable soft patch of earth, they dig a hole under the ball with their strong front legs and bury it. When deep enough the female lays an egg inside it. Later, when the grub hatches it finds itself surrounded by food which is enough for it until ready to pupate. This it does within what is left of the ball. Later it will emerge as an adult beetle.

Butterflies of the open bush are not spectacular and mostly grass yellows, blues and various whites, and in the tents of stillness to the lee of bushes, brown satyrs flop up and down, their dusky wings branded with small orange ringlets.

One of the commonest insects in the bush must be the tiny cocktail ant which lives in such profusion in the galls of every living whistling thorn, and which swarms out busily whenever a twig is touched. Perhaps they help prevent ruthless over-browsing of individual trees, by keeping browsers on the move.

A strange animal of the bush, the aardvark depends upon termites. There is something romantic, and almost mythical, about it, and just to know that aardvarks are really there, out in the night, adds a happy ingredient to our lives. Although we see them only occasionally, and only at night, we are always struck by their speed and grace, despite their bulky build. Everywhere there is evidence of their activity: both shallow and deep holes in the rains, and chains of their odd three-slot

Scarab

Large dung-beetle
with ball.

scarab beetles
rolling their ball of
dung.

Ball of elephant-dung
made by large elephant-
dependant dung beetle

Life size

Thomson's Gazelle (Gazella thomsoni)

Thomson's gazelle's horn. ♂.

Courtship chase in male's territory.

Aardvark

ted tracks. I think that their digging in hard ground provide inlets for rainwater, forming minute surface dams all over the plains, and conduits for guiding the water deeper below the surface. Their burrows also provide homes for foxes, jackals, hyaenas, warthogs, porcupines and aardwolves. All can dig for themselves but aardvarks are the champion diggers of them all, managing in a very short time what it might take the others days to achieve.

We were told of an aardvark that had been raised on a bottle, who became so affectionate that she would gambol and cavort with excitement and pleasure like a dog whenever her people returned after a short absence. It does not surprise me that sighting an aardvark is thought to bring good luck by some tribes.

Lions are said to be fond of aardvark flesh, and we have found the remains of two that had been killed and eaten by them.

Although the aardvark digs feeding holes wherever there are termites, the places that seem most full of their burrows are the open, treeless tops of the ridges. These windy, curved plains of shortly nibbled grass, so high in the clean air and with such sweeping views all around, are also home for the waggle-tailed Thomson's gazelles.

When Guy first came to Nyamuluki in 1963 there were no Thomson's gazelles. This was probably because the country was far more heavily bushed then, with extensive stands of whistling thorn. 'Tommies' are happiest on open plains and in glades where they can keep a distance from visible predators and make use of their considerable speed in evading them, and

mating.

female.

Baby stotting after mother.

Grant's gazelle (*Gazella grantii*)
on the central plain. Dry weather, noon.

they enjoy the short sweet grass that grows on the open ridge tops. The country of Nyamuluki has become steadily more open and suited to Tommies in the last eighteen years, perhaps owing to a combination of heavy browsing by giraffes and goats (now much reduced) and a series of dry years and droughts.

Another antelope of the open bush and one which seems happy in the driest weather, is the graceful Grant's gazelle. They often 'stot', that is, bounce along with all four legs held stiffly together, as if attached to invisible pogo-sticks. The effect of this is enchanting, as if the animals have suddenly become animated by Walt Disney. Stotting is used when evading danger, either real or imagined, and particularly at the beginning of the chase. It has been suggested that it may act as an advertisement to the predator: 'Look, I am so fit I can do this! It is no good chasing me'.

Impala have a 'double-stot', used occasionally when, after a huge bounce into the air, they come down on their front legs and do another smaller bounce, while the hind legs are still high above their heads. Then the hind legs drop down and they do another miraculous bounce into the air, repeat the process. The whole extraordinary movement is executed in an easy, floating manner. We have seen this action when the impalas are escaping from danger, and also when the does have been playing together. Occasionally an impala buck will bounce twice on his hind legs, especially when he wants to keep an eye on something low over the horizon.

The long-horned Beisa oryx are among the most decorative and exciting antelopes on Nyamuluki. When alarmed and galloping, they have a curious way of moving together, like a shoal of fishes or a flock of flying waders, that I do not remember seeing in any other mammal. The Kenya hartebeeste, a race that lives only on the Laikipia Plateau, is the fastest mammal on earth and has incredible stamina. Their action, which looks entirely effortless, as if golden dream rocking-horses are somehow floating through the bush at speed, appears to be miraculously economic of energy. In spite of their extraordinary, elongated faces, I think they are among the most thoroughbred looking of the antelopes, with their fine, clean limbs, silken skin and speedy, sloping build.

During and after the rains eland, the biggest of all antelopes, move in from surrounding areas till they are wading in the sweet plentiful grass in herds of several hundred, the great grey bulls towering above the tawny females. They carry their size and weight at an easy, swinging trot, their round black

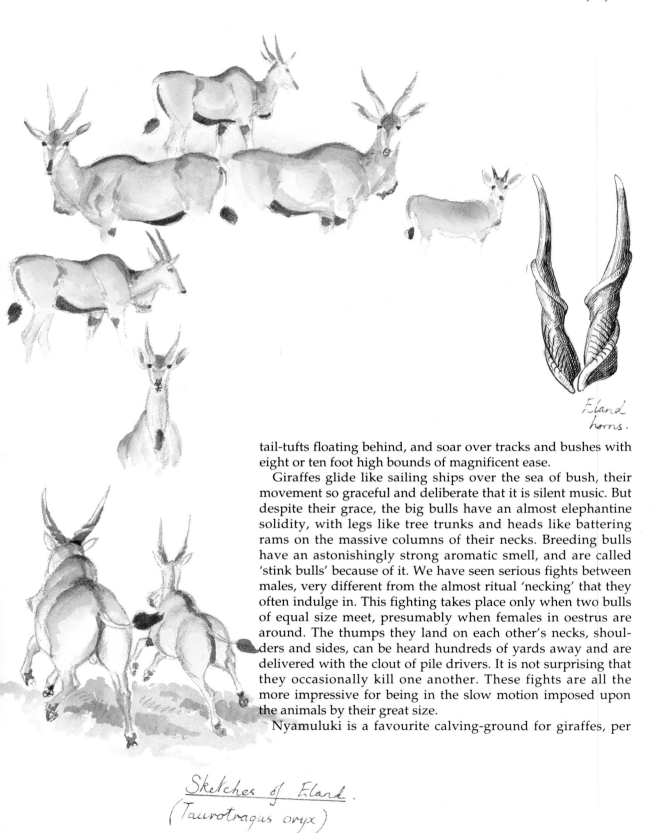

Eland horns.

tail-tufts floating behind, and soar over tracks and bushes with eight or ten foot high bounds of magnificent ease.

Giraffes glide like sailing ships over the sea of bush, their movement so graceful and deliberate that it is silent music. But despite their grace, the big bulls have an almost elephantine solidity, with legs like tree trunks and heads like battering rams on the massive columns of their necks. Breeding bulls have an astonishingly strong aromatic smell, and are called 'stink bulls' because of it. We have seen serious fights between males, very different from the almost ritual 'necking' that they often indulge in. This fighting takes place only when two bulls of equal size meet, presumably when females in oestrus are around. The thumps they land on each other's necks, shoulders and sides, can be heard hundreds of yards away and are delivered with the clout of pile drivers. It is not surprising that they occasionally kill one another. These fights are all the more impressive for being in the slow motion imposed upon the animals by their great size.

Nyamuluki is a favourite calving-ground for giraffes, per

Sketches of Eland.
(Taurotragus oryx)

Sketches of
Kenya Hartebeeste

Variation in chest stripes.

Mare with two of her daughters.

Some have "Shadow" stripes, but most here do not.

Sketches of Common (Burchell's) Zebras. (Equus burchelli granti).

haps because the rolling nature of the country gives females good visiblity over wide distances so that enemies can be spotted while still far away. In the past we sometimes saw groups of over a hundred together. But now that much of the bush has been replaced by grassland, giraffe numbers have decreased as they have moved elsewhere. With the advent of wetter years recently it appears that the bush is returning, and with it, perhaps, the giraffes.

Of all the mammals of Nyamuluki the commonest are horses. There are sometimes nearly two thousand of them when the grass is green, fewer in the dry weather; but they are always present, those little striped horses, the common zebras. I think they keep down the tough bamboo grass, thus allowing palatable new shoots to grow for the cattle. Without them the vegetation might steadily get coarser and less palatable, though many ranches look upon them simply as rivals to cattle. Each one is said to eat three times the amount that a cow eats. By keeping the grass short they also make fires more controllable and reduce losses from this serious dry weather threat.

In nature, zebras move when they have eaten the grass down. Unfortunately, a rancher on a place such as Nyamuluki cannot move his cattle, so he is left at the onset of the dry weather with less grass for them than would have been available were there fewer zebra. The cattle, not being able to move off, prevent that resting period for the land that would have occured naturally, and do much harm by overgrazing and trampling. This might seem to indicate that it would be better not to have cattle and to ranch wild animals, on a seasonal basis only, instead. But this is fraught with difficulty, for it would be hard to work out policies for ranchers and landowners concerning a wandering stock that would belong to them all equally, or to none at all. Who would make use of what? How much? When? As soon as wild animals are fenced and unable to wander freely, they become, in effect, domestic animals, and heir to the same troubles such as over stocking, inbreeding, disease and parasites, and need to be 'managed' as cattle are. Perhaps the best answer, and one that the pastoral tribes of Africa adopted, is for people and cattle to be nomadic also, but it seems that this way of life is increasingly frowned on and difficult to follow in a modern world.

White is by far the most efficient colour for throwing off heat from the sun, as we discovered when feeling the backs of our variously coloured horses. But it is also very conspicuous, so few wild animals here are white, though zebra have experimented successfully with it. Their black stripes break up that whiteness and not only prevent zebras from being conspicuous, but from a distance create a lovely scintillating grey that in some lights and in some settings, renders them almost invisible. Near to, the effect of many jazzily striped animals galloping together could be momentarily confusing to a predator. So the stripiness of zebras is yet another way in which nature explores all possible variations, in camouflage and heat dispersal, as in everything else.

In 1973 we saw the first Grévy's zebra on Nyamuluki. She was a thin, old mare who soon afterwards died of old age. The next year there were twelve; since then they have gradually increased, and recently we counted sixty. They have moved in from the north and seem to find Nyamuluki to their liking. Larger and superficially horse-like, they move like donkeys to whom they are more closely related than common zebras. A Grévy's voice is a long basso-profundo growl, ending in some comical squeaks and whistles, whereas a common zebra's is a musical yapping, or gruff barking (depending on how close the zebra is), and it is one of the most typical sounds of the bush. We hear it nearly every day and often at night.

It is not true, though often said, that 'one never sees a thin zebra'. We have seen many very thin zebras during droughts, and even at other times some of them are not fat, particularly yearlings and old mares. Stripes, though, mask the lean shapes making them appear rounded.

Lions like eating zebras and follow them onto Nyamuluki. Not long ago our daughters, who were seeing how close they could get on foot to a herd of zebras without disturbing them, noticed two 'brown animals' sitting behind a bush about forty yards away. At that moment, the lions (as they proved to be) jumped up and dashed in among the zebras. These scattered and Laria and Isabella heard a zebra scream as it was caught and killed behind a screen of nearby bushes.

The herdsmen of Nyamuluki meet lions not infrequently, and have had many anxious moments when lions have stampeded cattle out of their thornbush 'bomas' at night, or jumped in after them. One herdsman with each herd is armed with a shotgun which can be fired off into the air on such occasions, and this usually frightens the lions away.

Another efficient hunter of Nyamuluki, and one that, in spite of its reputation, is often conspicuously lacking in cowardice, is the spotted hyaena. They are formidable not only for their teeth, which are as big or bigger than those of a lion, and the great strength of their jaws (a female once tore her way out of the steel mesh of our box trap) but also for their intelligence,

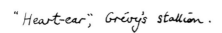

"Heart-ear", Grévy's stallion.

Grévy's Zebras.
(Equus grevyi).

Grévy's zebra foal.

Mare

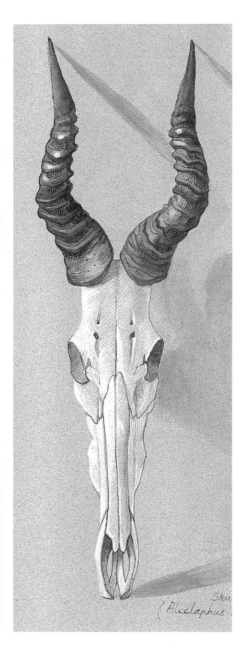

Sku
(Alcelaphus)

upon which many a thwarted rancher and farmer has commented, when his poison baits, ambushes and traps have been spurned.

We do not very often see hyaenas themselves, but their large tracks and chalky droppings are always to be found on the pathways and plains.

On Nyamuluki, hyaenas do not usually move in the packs that they often form elsewhere, but prefer to forage singly. There have been many times over the years when they have pushed under the wire-netting of a night *boma* to seize a sheep or goat, often killing or wounding others with those incredibly strong jaws in the excitement of the moment, and sometimes causing the whole flock to break outside in a panic. For this reason a dog is kept at each *boma* to warn of their presence and that of other potential stock thieves. Any animal left outside at night has always been fair game to the hyaena, but on the whole we have been at peace with each other, and their strange and evocative calls have always been part of our night. When a hyaena sends series of these powerful sounds through the darkness, it hangs its head low between its front legs, most unlike a dog or wolf. There is something lonely and prehistoric about the sound, and also disquieting. Perhaps it stirs memories from the time when our ancestors had not made themselves so secure from predators, and when large packs of hyaenas could have been a great danger, as they still are occasionally to modern man.

It was only when we were box-trapping spotted hyaenas for a National Park that we became aware that these were striped hyaenas on Nyamuluki, for we caught two on different parts of the ranch. They were quiet and docile in the trap, whereas the spotted hyaenas were restless and growled. Both kinds, however, displayed sense and strong nerves, showing no symptoms of panic or undue anxiety, unlike the leopards that were also translocated. These seemed to suffer extremes of anxiety which they tried, pathetically, to hide under a show of ferocity.

The striped hyaena is a quieter and more solitary animal than the spotted, and extremely well camouflaged. So well did the coats of the two we caught blend with their background, that for a few seconds I thought the trap was empty.

While hyaenas seem to be in no danger of disappearing, the cheetah, a specialised speed machine, is, together with the Cape hunting dog, an animal for which we feel anxiety. It has always been a regular visitor to Nyamuluki and references to it in my diaries over the last twenty years have been numerous. We once had, for a few weeks, a group of eight cheetahs together, and sometimes we have seen parties of six or seven, which for cheetahs is considered unusual. Females have raised their cubs on the ranch, some of them dying of starvation or disease, and others growing up to be the splendid, heraldic beauties which are amongst the most exciting animals to be seen in the wild. I suppose they have hunted over this land, taking animals up to the size of weaner eland, for thousands of years. But in the last three years there have been fewer of them, though we still find their tracks here and there, and see them occasionally.

Apart from predators, dangers to stock in the bush of Nyamuluki include snake bite, particularly that of the puff-adder. Murray skinned one of only two feet long, when it had been killed after biting seven sheep in quick succession as they came to inspect it. Three of the sheep died, but the others recovered. Then there was the evening that Jake, an Australian blue-heeler dog, and I, were running down a rocky bare slope to one of the dams. There was a sudden blur of movement and in that same split second Jake made a small skip, and so avoided being bitten by a large puff-adder. It was marvellously camouflaged, and if it had not moved I do not think we would have noticed it. It lay coiled in upon itself, puffed up, its triangular, blunt-nosed head raised an inch from the ground and drawn back ready if necessary to strike again. It watched us tremble, while its black tongue slipped in and out trying to get our scent. It must have been over five inches in diameter, and well over four feet long. Recently we measured another of four feet eleven inches, and they sometimes reach a much greater size.

Sometimes I think that we must pass many puff-adders in the grass without noticing them, and that they simply draw back their heads and let us go by unscathed. It would be a waste of venom to bite so large an animal as a human unless the snake was actually being trodden on.

Cobras seem to be peaceful unless stirred up, though we have had a few stock deaths attributed to them. Two examples of this 'non-aggression' come to mind. One was when a herdsman, getting into his blankets for the night, felt a snake moving in them. He jumped up and upon shaking out the blankets found a cobra. The cobra neither bit him nor spat, but was nevertheless killed in spite of its forbearance. The other incident was when I was walking in long grass and nearly tripped over the tail of a seven-foot cobra which had been sunbathing. It whipped to and fro in a frantic attempt to escape, and at my cry of alarm one of the dogs made a grab for its tail, luckily

*Prehistoric handaxes
from Handaxe Gully.*

missing. The cobra made off without threatening us. I can think of many other occasions when one or other of us, or the dogs or horses, came close to cobras and they did nothing but move away. If they feel themselves threatened seriously they may, of course, react in the formidable way that is so often expected of them.

Much more dangerous to the cattle on Nyamuluki than either predator or snake, is the tick, because of the fatal diseases it carries. The message of the tick seems to be: 'cattle are not suited to this land. They do not fit in. They are unbalancing its systems. Disease must either eliminate or adapt them.' But we have an economic interest in cattle, so we interfere with a battery of medicines and needles. We have our own idea about the most useful shape and type that cattle should be, and in our selective breeding may work for a different beast than the one that nature might finally select. But in the end, all nature's ploys and gambits, even disease, work for the maintenance of diversity and equilibrium, and for maximum productivity.

Man has lived on Nyamuluki for thousands, no a million years, as we know from the evidence he has left. Below one of the dam spillways, overflow in the rains washes ancient hand-axes out of the ground. As you pick one up and feel it fit comfortably into your hand, as all good tools should fit, it is almost as if someone from those days long ago has reached out his hand and touched yours: a feeling of communion with a far, far distant past that for a magic second melds with your own present. Perhaps that axe once helped to skin one of the great mammals of the Pleistocene.

Less ancient are the worked chips of jet-black obsidian or volcanic glass which we find everywhere on Nyamuluki. A source of the sharpest cutting edges, the obsidian from which the chips were worked must have been brought from the Rift Valley, for it does not occur naturally here. And on some of the ridges there are pink granite boulders that have been rubbed until they are as smooth and cool to feel as polished marble. This was done by generations of Maasai sharpening their spears and *simis* (swords) on them. In recent historical times, the people grazed their cattle on Nyamuluki and over the whole of the Laikipia Plateau of which it is part.

There is no more lovely sight for me than the plains of Nyamuluki dotted thickly with zebras, herds of eland, floating giraffes, red cattle and golden hartebeeste; where man has lived harmoniously from the Stone Age until now. Yet despite this long tenure I know that man could make the intricate webs of life those folds of land support could disappear almost as

Tick birds on a Boran bull.

the morning mist rises, and floats, and vanishes.

I hope that centuries hence there will still be those sounds which, almost more than anything else, evoke a place in one's mind. The simple, slightly wistful, and repeated song of the rufous-naped lark is the epitome of the open bush-dotted plains of Nyamuluki. The strident, echoing calls of the Senegal bustard on a moonlit night symbolise all that is wild and time-less about it. But one of the most lovely 'sounds' of all, which overlies all others on Nyamuluki, is the silence. That silence, punctuated by the calls and songs of birds and the breath of the wind in the whistling thorns, has taken the place of music for me. Perhaps music is, after all, man's attempt at expressing that infinitely grand something that seems to be heard in the silence of a living wilderness, if you listen hard enough.

Speckled Sulphur-tip
Colotis agoye.

a large wood white.
Leptosia medusa..?.
(Prefers shade, shelter from wind)

acrea acrita.
Fiery acrea. ♀

Belenois zochalia
Forest white. ♀.

Orange and
lemon
Eronia leda.
(Near river)

Painted lady
Vanessa cardui.

Mocker Swallowtail ♂
Papilio dardanus.

Yellow Pansy ♂
Precis hierta.
(very common. Settles on ground.)

April '89. Rains.

Sketch from House-dam Ridge looking towards the Mountain (hidden in cloud). Afternoon.
Whistling thorn (Acacia drepanolobium), Bamboo grass (Pennisetum straminium), Boscia trees.

Almost the same view painted on a clear evening. December '90. Dry weather